For HNC,
in memoriam

89
Collana **Alleli / Research**

ISBN 978-88-6242-588-9

First edition March 2022

Cover design: Francesco Trovato
Book design: Gaetano Salemi

LetteraVentidue Edizioni S.r.l.
Via Luigi Spagna 50 P
96100 Siracusa, Italy

www.letteraventidue.com

conrad-bercah

MODERNISM: AN AMERICAN WAKE.

a personal anthology:
1997-2020

LetteraVentidue

Two Greeks converse: perhaps Socrates and Parmenides.
It is best if we never know their names; in that way the story will be simpler and more mysterious. The theme of the dialogue is abstract. They sometimes allude to myths, in which they both disbelieve. The reasons they allege may abound in fallacies and they do not come to a conclusion.

They do not polemicize. And they do not want to persuade or be persuaded: they do not think in terms of winning or losing. They are in agreement on a single point: they know that discussion is the not-impossible way to find a truth. Free of myth and metaphor, they think or attempt to think.

We shall never know their names. This conversation between two unknowns someplace in Greece is the capital event in History. They have forgotten prayer and magic.

Jorge Louis Borges, *The Beginning.*

Contents

PRELIMINARY REMARKS

A personal American wake

Berlin, 2020

In the summer of 1996, I was asked by Harry Cobb to help him envision a book planned to mark the fifty-year anniversary of the practice that his former partner, I.M. Pei, had founded in New York City in 1948. Due to the season—summertime—the arrangement of our first meeting turned out to be a prolonged affair. So did the decision to undertake the project. Both instances may be recalled now as emblematic of our subsequent activity, namely the extended search for a suitable format to arrange Cobb's work—the problem being the discomfort Cobb exhibited from day one in having intimate parts of his personal, professional and intellectual biography made available to the public in the form of a book. Half-jokingly, Isaiah Berlin used to describe himself as an intellectual taxi of sorts, because he had to be hailed like a taxi in order to write something. This is an apt description of the way architectural work is produced, and it surely is an appropriate description of the way Cobb's mind worked. In consequence, the reader may identify the present author as the driver who was supposed to 'bring Cobb to town,' so to speak.

The question 'Why, of all people, should I become the driver?' is best answered as follows: because I happened to be around when the time was ripe. Simply stated, in order to fulfil the requirement of a thesis project to be discussed at the Harvard Design School, I had written a somewhat lengthy theoretical inquiry discussing three values that I had deemed important to implement throughout my own career, being an architect who was stepping into the professional world. As it happened, one of them stemmed from discussing a predicament that is neglected by almost all but a few people: the TOB (Tall Office Building) predicament. Since Cobb is one of those few individuals, since my speculation caught his attention, and, finally, since the fifty-year anniversary was hailing him, all of the above proved to be a combination that was sufficiently exciting to undertake such an uncertain project—in many ways it was a two-year-long cab ride headed towards a constantly changing and unknown destination. The only thing that was not subject to change was the time of the ride: Saturday mornings in the silent rooms of Cobb's Madison Avenue office in mid-town Manhattan.

Literally bursting with excitement, armed with a long list of probing questions and a tape recorder, I threw myself into each and every ride. I occasionally changed roles—from passenger to driver, then to passenger again, etcetera—but always trying to get my interlocutor, who had never previously had an interest in releasing information about his practice in a consistent way, to talk about the nuts and bolts in the mechanism of his mind, and explain the ups and downs of his career. It took me a few Saturdays to understand the complexity of the business at hand. What emerged, as our talks began, was a sort of striking contrast between the two speaking voices that seemed difficult to overcome. To start, the mood was quite different. Being a young Turk finding his footing with no knowledge of the dreariness of the material's reality, I was looking at the TOB problem as a challenge and therefore felt passionate about it. Cobb, having spent half a century dealing with it, understood the issue more as a problematic situation than anything else. Therefore he felt the opposite of passionate about it. Secondly, he expressed scepticism quite early in the game regarding the usefulness of general statements to be made about architecture. Thirdly, he wanted me to provide an 'interesting misrepresentation' of his professional life. The only item we agreed upon it seemed was the fact that architectural theory had little, if anything, to do with the image of it that could be formed in one's mind from participating in academic activities, particularly in North America. In the end, after a lot of back and forth, a 'deal' was reached with apparent mutual satisfaction: the edited transcription of a week-long conversation would ultimately be deemed the best format to introduce the unique architecture of his mind. The format presented the advantage of being an offshoot of a glorious precedent that Cobb found pertinent enough to be comfortable with when I brought it to his attention. This was the Hitchcock/Truffaut conversations during which a young Truffaut 'forced' the revered Hitchcock to talk about his films to make a number of insights available to the public concerning cinematic questions that came from a director who was widely misunderstood back then, to put it mildly. If this was not by the public at large, it was so at least by the so-called educated, or more 'brainy' audiences in the field.

I shall presently confess that I have always understood my role in the enterprise in a similar fashion because Cobb's own thinking about architecture had never been the subject of widespread attention. Just as the aim of Truffaut was to modify the way critics approached Hitchcock's work, I thought at the time that a book featuring a conversation between a young architect and a mature, respected one may aspire to achieve a not so dissimilar condition. In addition, it could set the record straight for once.[1]

---

1. The 'deal' failed to translate into immediate publication, which Cobb had resisted from the get-go at any rate, as if somebody was forcing his hand against him. The material and his missing 'interesting misrepresentation' had therefore remained hidden somewhere inside of Cobb's psyche for twenty years. It was eventually released (2018) in a heavily mutilated form that washed out most of

A quarter of a century later, I believe that I have acquired the serenity to retrospectively admit the sheer recklessness of the project. How can it be possible to think that a recent graduate, coming from a completely different cultural and linguistic background, has the required skills to find an appropriate format to present a figure in architecture while directly dealing with the living subject of his work? A subject who was supposed to have a final say on everything?

I mentioned some of the differences earlier that stood between us. However, I forgot to mention the most evident one, namely the significant age difference. When we first met, he was seventy years old, while I was in my late twenties and wondering why he wanted to converse with me. Fairly soon, it became apparent that 'dialogue' was the key word and that the value of having a dialogue trumped the demands of a having a book published. A man in constant Socratic dialogue, at times quarrelling with himself, endlessly questioning and shifting his mental position, and glad to have a sparring partner, Cobb was just looking for someone to deliver his inner conversations to himself. Oddly enough, a more obvious issue escaped me: the potential influence on my own outlook on architecture. I discovered that influence in the years that followed this exchange, whose regularity came to an end at the end of 1998, some twenty years before the end of Cobb's own life. He passed away in the final weeks of winter on March 9, 2020 at a rather interesting juncture in time, when the global virus that has stopped the world was about to land on American shores. It is well known that the virus

its inconvenient 'truths,' specifically the ones tearing off some of the most hypocritical masks of the corporate world in which Cobb spent his life.

has managed to effortlessly perform an unthinkable job no one foresaw: lift the lid of *omertà* that has kept the stunning U-turn of the American spirit in the gutter for about a quarter of a century, and discard values Cobb himself spent a lifetime naturally swimming in. It is this new condition and the liberating energy brought with it that have prompted the release of what follows, specifically an attempt to 'abandon' an activity that has been keeping me company intermittently for over two decades. It is an activity that brackets my working relationship with Cobb, both pre-dating and following it. It is also a rather unpopular activity: penning notes about some of the cultural issues reflected in American modernism and its discontents, such as the influence it has historically been playing on the theory and practice of architecture, shaping the way they are now both understood in increasing portions of the non-English-speaking world, which is now increasingly and alarmingly mimicking the English-speaking one to the former's own detriment.

The fact that this specific activity has been with me for such a long time is arguably the consequence of a largely circumstantial (unplanned, that is) trans-Atlantic *Ausbildung*. It was gathered in three stages in three cities—Milan, New York and Berlin—that are still as diverse as their respective languages and religious traditions. They have remained substantially indifferent to the rhetoric of globalization and the supporting activity of its (thoughtless) sponsors, who are (still continuing) to play no minor role in how architectural form is perceived, understood and used.[2]

---

2. The remarks of this preliminary note reflect the belief, expressed by Giacomo Marramao, that the contingent is the most useful ontological category to talk about the contemporary, because it shows a clear dissatisfaction with the

Having experienced it, I can say that if there is an advantage to having practiced the profession (admitting that being involved with the architectural form is indeed a 'profession') in such diverse places (which I do not recommend) is to find oneself in the unique position of being a third-party observer. By living in these places, an understanding of it has been formed that is more based on life experience than on academic literature about life. There is an understanding that results from having to face the problem of coming to terms with cultures that stem from completely different and, at times, opposing value systems. Because of their differences, they appear to the newcomer in terms that are arguably sharper than to those observers who do not have the challenge of facing this kind of problem.[3]

---

linear notion of temporality expressed by modernism, which aspires precisely to forget the fundamental role that contingency plays in historical evolution. I consider the improbable and unplanned to be the real fabric of the 'carpet' identifying the time of an architectural form, that is, the fabric in which the energy necessary to clarify the historical index is stored. Post litteram, that index allows us to understand the causes and role of randomness, which is unique from contingency, and they should not be confused. Having said this, I also confess to being convinced, thanks to real life experiences, that chance remains an unavoidable factor for those who work as architects.

3. All pieces collected in what follows implement a number of theses hosted in the unique philosophy of history formulated by Giovanni Battista Vico some time ago to challenge traditional assumptions about the universality of methods and values across the globe and throughout history. Vico made a convincing case showing how, no matter what Voltaire thought and preached, on the contrary, a cultural pluralism is in place in the world. This pluralism is a reflection of a variety of cultures that pursue different, and often incompatible ways of life, ideals, standards and values. Within this panorama, each culture expresses itself in works of art, thoughts, life styles and politics. Each one possesses its own character which does not necessarily form a combinable stage of a single type of progress toward a universally shared goal. There is a view that entails there

Yet, I also now fully realize that the inner dialogue that Cobb needed actually kept happening sporadically for over twenty years in a different body. It was the body of the driver/interlocutor in a collection of different documents in different formats—articles, journal entries, essays, profiles, personal impressions—that entertain an oblique but fascinating relationship with the original book project. In fact, at this point I think that the material has gained a somewhat 'archaeological' interest for the reader as well as the author who sees a single option in order to move on from it: abandon it to its own destiny. Perhaps someone else will find it sufficiently stimulating in the near or distant future to eventually interact with some of its facets which have been pushed out the window in the meantime by the prevailing rhetoric of the day: the relentless techno-fetishism now deployed on a massive scale to mask an irreversible submission to market forces that thrive on making a marketable spectacle of architectural form either by resorting to specious naturalism or deviated engineering. Or both.

A few words on the subject are arguably needed. Some of the points made in the texts are occasionally reworked

---

be no room in the arts for any talk about 'progress,' as each culture creates masterpieces that belong solely to it. It is a view that is still valid today, in spite of the gargantuan scale of the action performed the by the tech companies of Silicon Valley to create one single man the world over. The material gather in the anthology stems from this philosophy as well as its most important corollary: that a great deal of fantasia is needed when dealing with the past because, without it, the past remains dead. To bring it back to life, one needs to attempt to enter into the minds of people who lived in bygone eras, try to listen to their arguments, being both overt and covert, and conjecture what their intentions might have been. This is an operation which is only available to the people who have first-hand knowledge of the culture they are investigating.

or repeated. Some of the documents themselves may appear, as they do to the present writer, as too 'enthusiastic,' or an overly optimistic reflection on the often unjustifiable, if not groundless, optimism of youth. The reader will understand that these 'shortcomings' are perhaps due to the zeal of an author who was too young, and the fact that it is difficult to avoid repetition or discrepancies in such a prolonged amount of time. Yet they are being printed so they can contribute to the reflections on the one tonality that is today perceived as urgently necessary because of its sheer, loud absence: the need for self-doubt about the very virus with which the rhetoric of modernism has invested architectural form and which began exactly a century ago. This virus can perhaps be best recapped in the following manner: the virulence of arrogant radicals who consider themselves rightly equipped to address the future of the coming society, specifically the society that a hundred years later is still unable to shake off (modernist) rhetoric.

It is a tonality expressed by those who, like the present writer, find little help in the prevailing rhetoric of the day. Like Isaiah Berlin did, they still think that to be human is to communicate with other human beings in a non-digital fashion, without the buffer of social media, that is. And more importantly, they still believe that architectural form should not be turned into a marketable silhouette that is ready to be sold as a vehicle for mass-communication. This is for the very simple reason that architecture can only be a difficult art, or a form or resistance, whose job is precisely to provide a critique of both historical materialism and/or deviated liberalism. It is a form of resistance that carries traces of its difficult relationship with non-chronological notions of time, more precisely, the notions of time that are not forced by the digital compulsion of the day. It is a concept of time that can unmask the foolishness of the hysterical optimism of old and new fundamentalists of modernism alike. In other words, it is an idea of time that can plant permanent question marks in the path of all generalizations, like the linear belief of time that modernism injected into the body of the discipline of architecture exactly a century ago.[4]

The material gathered in the anthology that follows is then made of different fabrics in which the personal and impersonal are interwoven. There are reasons to see it as a personally critical eulogy for a personal 'presence' that has now literally turned into a more 'ghostly' version. Yet, it can also be seen as a way of providing a personal *Nachleben* (after-life) to a latent material whose 'hour of readability' (as Walter Benjamin himself would have expressed it) has arguably come.[5] Such *Nachleben* presents the added

---

4. Cfr. the inquiry that Giacomo Marramao carried out on the political categories of modernity to propose a symbolic-genealogical reconstruction of them in a trilogy on time: *Potere e secolarizzazione. Le categorie del tempo*, (Torino: Editori Riuniti, 1983); *Minima temporalia. Tempo, spazio, esperienza* (Milano: Il Saggiatore, 1990) *Kairós. Apologia del tempo debito*, (Torino: Bollati Boringhieri, 2020). As Marramao himself points out, today 'the future no longer appears, as it did at the time of the industrial revolution, to be a liberating dimension, but an innovative routine removed from the will of individual subjects and delegated to impersonal technological structures.' Time, in other words, no longer seems 'at our disposal' but appears more and more as an a priori that Western rationalism and the logic of the market tyrannizes over our lives thanks to a 'mephistophelian' welding between the technology of 'real time' with incessant and pressing digital needs in which the means have become ends, heedless of the needs and timing of the 'end users,' now stunned by a neurotic and, indeed, pathological 'presentism' in which any notion of future or planning has annihilated any elaboration of our past.

5. For Benjamin, the hour of readability is the appropriate time that every material has grafted in its body as if it was a historical index, or an appropriate time

advantage of continuing the dialogue, having agreed that a 'discussion is the not-impossible way to find a truth, without thinking in terms of winning or losing.'[6]

'Once a modernist, always a modernist,' Cobb told me during one of our conversations. This was to indicate the irreversibility of a frame of mind that is arguably justified by its own uncompromising radicalism. One that (and this is remarkable) did not prevent him from becoming a reasonable critic of it, and planting a number of permanent question marks in both its body and *geist*. Unfortunately, it is an attitude that is largely absent today, when it is actually needed most. This attitude is required to effectively counter the current *poltergeist* that has captured American civilization (and its academia): the inability to maintain a distance from an information technology that makes it impossible to still appreciate the still crucial difference between an urn and a chamber-pot. Even more alarming, it allows them to be confused, resorting to a chamber-pot when an urn is needed in reality. It is for this very reason

---

to be understood or consumed, as if it was yogurt. The notion is at the base of his idiosyncratic 'quotation style' that does not aim to make the reader relive a fragment of the past but, on the contrary, intends to use the dialectical power of the quotation itself detached from its original context to establish a renewed relationship with the reader. It is a dialectical power capable of bringing together an instant from the past and one from the present in a new 'constellation' where the present can aspire to clarify the message of the past which, in turn, therefore experiences the materialization of the appropriate time (kairos) of its readability, i.e. the time which Benjamin's thesis explains is inscribed in its historical index.

6. Cfr. the Epigraph. Dialogue was proclaimed by Bakhtin to be the ultimate form of human self-expression, a form which existed in flux and was subject to open-ended questioning by a free mind. John Dewey famously said that 'democracy begins in conversations.'

that I have come to consider the material gathered in the anthology that follows as my personal and 'reversed' American wake for the frame of mind that has shaped Cobb's life and is still very much alive: American modernism and its ever-present discontent which, contrary to both in the spirit and the letter of the law of Irish wakes, I hope the world will learn to forget in a much overdue *requiem* before it is too late.[7]

---

7. An American wake is a term originating in rural Ireland in the 1800s at a time of poverty and famine, when emigration to America meant a one-way ticket and never seeing your family again. Since many emigrants were leaving behind a life of poverty, the 'American wake' represented a last chance to ever hear from a departing man or woman. The emigrant was heading into a life of uncertainty and there was no guarantee that they would ever be able to communicate with their family again. The American Wake was therefore the chance for many to say a last goodbye to family and friends as it usually happens in wakes. American wakes were extremely melancholic affairs. Women renowned for their ability to lament were invited to the wakes to give emotional eulogies about the departing emigrant. They traditionally delivered the eulogies in a high-pitched wail, resulting in rooms full of crying women and weeping men. An American wake is therefore quite similar to a funeral wake, except for one key difference; the person having a wake is still alive. Like modernism is.

Henry N. Cobb: A Profile

New York City, 1999. Unpublished

The following piece is a sort of cross between a New Yorker-style profile and a eulogy, namely a piece of writing in praise of a person delivered on special occasions like birthdays, office parties, retirement celebrations or a funeral. If this explains its praising tone, it does not explain why it was written in 1999. Eulogies are usually delivered by a family member or a close family friend in the case of a death, while a living eulogy (given at monumental moments such as retirement) is recited by a senior colleague. Not being either, I see this eulogy twenty years later as either a personal way of putting a stone over a book project, or (in journalistic jargon) a 'crocodile'—a commemorative, pre-packaged article on the life of a well-known personage which is created to be published as soon as the news of the person's death is made public, showing the importance of the deceased. So, in a way, this stands now as a personal 'wake' in honor of Cobb and is being delivered twenty years after it was written.

Henry N. Cobb, who may well be the least celebrated among the first rate American architects of our day, is a man in a hurry. He appears now to have gone through life in a state of perpetual conflict with time—a status perhaps common to many Newyorkers. Though a Bostonian by birth and by education, Cobb has in fact so far spent two third of his life living in New York City—which Truman Capote once compared to the experience of living through the tungsten of an electric bulb—working side by side with his partners, I. M. Pei and James Ingo Freed. There is no reason to believe that he will ever interrupt such activity; or that he will ever live anywhere but in New York City. This, of course, does not mean that Cobb seldom leaves New York City. Quite the contrary, his weeks are mostly spent in traveling back and forth between New York City and wherever the site of the project he is working on might be-an activity that has increased through the course of his career and that has accelerated in the last decade, reaching a frantic pace.

"I am busier than I have ever been" is one of the very first things that he told me when we first met. We had been in contact for a few weeks, discussing the possibility of working together on a section devoted to him within a monograph that was meant to celebrate the fiftieth anniversary of the architectural practice he cofounded—the Pei Cobb Freed partnership. The section devoted to him was in stagnant state, nobody really working on it, and therefore he was concerned about founding somebody who could do so, namely to get the project going—this is why our paths crossed.

"I would like you to propose different ways of presenting my work since I do not have the time nor the distance to do so. I myself know nothing about it other than it has to be an 'interesting misrepresentation' of it. It shall draw the reader to want to know more about it even though it should be modest in the posture. Unassuming" is how his intentions toward the document can be best summarized at the time when we first met at his office on Madison Avenue in New York City. At the same time, however, he handed me a copy of an essay written a hundred and six years before the above words were spoken. This was a survey of some of the processes by which a large building in Chicago evolved, "from the time when the site is determined to the time of its occupancy." Cobb thought the world of it and did not loose time in telling me the reason, which had to do with the absence of cultural name dropping and, above all, with the absence of everything else that so much characterizes the architectural bookshelf of the present day: architectural jargon, hyperbole and the exhibition of doctrinarism—undoubtedly one of the three aspects of life that he dislikes the most, the other being the frivolous display of human emotions and irony—two items that, I think, simply do not appear to sit well with his nature.

Uncertain, yet excited, the combination of all of the above made little sense to me at the time when it occurred. It makes more sense now that our undertaking has been carried through "somewhat successfully" as Cobb told me a few weeks ago in an almost incredulous tone. I will say later why this is so. For the time being, I am just interested in suggesting an opposition—one that perhaps help me to trace a profile of my interlocutor. I now in fact recall, thanks to hindsight, that time did not seem to be pressing the day Cobb and I first met; nor appeared to be so in our subsequent encounters, which took place on a number of Saturday and holidays mornings at his office where I would find him sitting at the short leg of his L-shaped wooden desk, making phone calls. My appearance would eventually be dignified by the stopping of his activity and is consequential self-relocation to the other leg of the desk where I would find him in front of me, ready to be helped to remember and to be asked about the various predicaments of his career.

A dignified, solemn gentleman with silvery hair, Cobb would wear in such occasions a much less formal outfit than his place in the world usually calls for: no tie, no pin-stripe suit, no formal postures even though his natural *denouement* would suffer no harm from it. "I hope you have something interesting to say, because I have nothing to say!" was a typical opening on his part—one that, when I first heard it increased my anxiety level—which was already high by any standard—but that eventually I managed to become accustomed to. What I also gradually had to get used to was a far more peculiar feature of his persona: namely, the measured tempo with which he delivers his thoughtful, always to the point, words. "That is the way I speak! I am sorry but you have to put up with it," Cobb said, speaking with no particular accent but particular slowness of speed and softness of voice—the one thing that even those who have had occasional contacts him and with whom I met in connection to my project have not failed to remark upon. What this profile is trying to single out is that such a fashion of speaking may also be a fashion of thinking, one that is important to exemply Cobb's singular way of being an architect. Cobb, in fact, is one of the few persons who means each and every one of their words-a tradition today mostly out of fashion. Within such small group, however, Cobb stands out, I think, in that, even if he is in a hurry, as he usually is, he never thinks twice about using his time in looking for the most appropriate word if he feels that such a word will help his interlocutor better grasp the point he is trying to make. This is why one can say that, while speaking, he usually assumes the air and the posture of a man who is not going to be rushed, taking whatever time he needs to align his words as if the latter were subject to an almost mathematical counting. When he is finished counting, he adds something else, occasionally introducing a different yet related topic. In short, a man in no hurry to finish his sentences—on the contrary, a man prodigal with words and time—an arrangement that parallels the painstaking, almost fastidious care that he takes for his buildings but, which, also, accounts for the curious opposition that I have just tried to sketch, namely the very meditative voice of a man in constant conflict with a schedule which, being frantic, one would naturally think leaves very little time for meditation. I will try to say why I think that important to understand the man and the architect in what follows.

Born in 1926, Cobb is in his own words "Boston born and bred." Raised according to New England's value system, raised to be a good man and do good in the world, that is, he grew up at a time of great economic and political uncertainty and fast developing evil—the 1930s—an age that no one could seriously consider any kind of model age. Although a Harvard-bred Bostonian by power of tradition, Cobb decided as a young man to challenge the set of values implied in that tradition with a simple, untraditional move: to take up the arts as a serious career. The architecture department was the one he felt passionate and, typically, anxious about. Some of the notes that I have accumulated about him register that the Exeter Academy's library is to be held responsible for both sentiments. The books it housed in fact, namely (with Cobb) "Giedion's electrifying manifesto Space, Time and Architecture and Frank Lloyd Wright's collected essays In the Cause of Architecture, lavishly nurtured" his passion and propel[led] him "headlong, and heedless of all else," onto what, typically, he perceived to be "the shortest possible path toward the practice of that art." This path was, in fact, the one designed by the Harvard GSD—Graduate School of Design—whose front door, being a member of the 1946 class of Harvard College, he entered the very same year—at age twenty, that is at a time when the widely spread American belief that "those interested in the arts should have gone to Paris" was arguably challenged for the first time—in architecture, for once ahead of the allied arts, at any rate.

The time and the mood are familiar enough: it was not long after Joseph Hudnut had established the new Harvard GSD, after Walter Gropius was said to have started to set architectural education into a relatively unprecedented fashion, after a socially concerned architecture had made its appearance in North America and, most of all, after Siegfried Giedion had gathered, in a written form, an unparalleled hoax to be played upon generations eager to be deceived, namely the so-called (by Giedion himself, at any rate) "third generation" of modern architects. The year 1946 was the time when all these things were, indeed, in full swing, their terrifying (overwhelming) power ready to be discovered in a matter of a few years by almost everybody, architects and the public at large. *Una tantum*, architects felt liberated from the tyranny of dead styles and, indeed, entitled, to put it as Cobb himself did, to devote themselves to the happy and progressive "joining together of art, technology, and social purpose for the benefit of humankind."

The point one should consider in this connection is that when Cobb was a student at Harvard a belief system was imposed upon he and his fellow classmates. Such system appears now to have rested on some basic assumptions—all of which determined the unquestionable criteria for assessing any work of architecture. These assumptions may be said to be the following: first of all, that only one logical solution was available to the architect of the day and that the solution was expected to come out by a genuine and correct stating of the problem. The solution, somehow, was already hidden in the program and the problems presented by each and every new commission. If this was not so, it had to do with the way the question was posed. Secondly, that the only method available to architects to operate—indeed the only method which was expected to lead to correct solutions—was rational in character and, in essence, identical for all building types. Thirdly, that solutions, being independent of the place in which commissioner required the buildings to take literally place, had to be true regardless of the location. In a way solutions were true for all places: New York or Brasilia was no difference. Such criteria, it has to be noticed, were curiously unrelated to traditional architectural terms. Strictly speaking, in fact, no room whatsoever was left for aesthetic concerns above the image-making function of architecture by what some have called a conspiracy of silence.

Such a three-legged stool of ethical duty was somehow held to be self-evident and it was further assumed to be the only rational way of building—a way responsive to the needs of what society was, or ought to be. To question this, to contrast developments which could not be otherwise, was to upset the triumphal march of history and, therefore, it had to be regarded as the doing of some antisocial and probably immoral member of society. "Art had to be integral with society." This was what Nikolaus Pevsner himself and many of his fellow travellers firmly stood for, believing that the New Style, "a genuine and adequate style of our century" had already been achieved by 1914—the year of

Gropius's Fagus Factory—the search for it having started in 1901, when "the work of all the pioneers began to converge into one universal movement." All of this, furthermore, was particularly evident in architectural writing—at Harvard more so than elsewhere—which tended to explain the new style of building as a consequence of something else, namely German theories of space and time which spread the populist notion that the architect of the time was but a mere will-deprived instrument of them.

Cobb graduated in 1949. A year later he took the first opportunity he had to separate himself from his *alma mater* and his hometown, both of which he regarded as impediments to the development of his career. The latter in particular appeared to him "economically moribund—an impression strengthened by the fact that no major commercial office building had been put up in it since 1912. "Only two big insurance companies had built new offices during my lifetime, and both, so it seemed to me, had done their best to forget that they were building in the twentieth century." One of the two buildings, in particular—the New England Life building in the Back Bay—is said to have helped him to perceive Boston, via David McCord, as "An urn burial that was best escaped before one was prematurely interred." Too hasty to come to terms with this, Cobb relocated himself to New York, having been invited to do so by his former Harvard mentor, I. M. Pei, who was then heading an unprecedented and, by the standard of the day, somehow illegal architectural task force patronized by the most cunning urban developer of the same day, William Zeckendorf.

Zeckendorf, having set his primary goal in life—to bring to new life forgotten urban environments—and having had been responsible for some bold and somehow self-promoted surgical operations on the more decayed parts of urban textures in as disparate parts of North America as Denver, Colorado and Montreal, Canada, helped both men to establish themselves in a matter of a few years as the principal exponents of such activity, satisfying urban appetites developed during their own student days. Their subsequent and collaborative practice may be said to have been an almost direct offspring of this beginning, its impact upon North American cities being of such magnitude that an historicization of it is certainly beyond the scope of the present piece, which, as mentioned earlier, is simply attempting to align a few considerations about Cobb's own way of being an architect—a way whose side value does not appear to be correctly evaluated.

Cobb thinks—and certainly told me so during two years of conversations together—of the John Hancock tower as the hinge upon which his professional life revolves. As told below, what I shall here suggest is that the Hancock odyssey can now be held responsible for having triggered a radical change in the path of his intellectual life, a change that would ultimately be formalized by the experience of going through an academic appointment at the Harvard GSD. There, although not warmly received at first because of the very education he received at the same institution some three decades earlier, he ultimately won the respect and the support of the entire community in his relentless effort of putting together a pedagogical program whose underlying construct—to instil into students the need to find themselves—was opposite to the one that characterized his education, which, on the contrary, was based on the need of instilling in the student body a prearranged body of all-embracing, all-explaining certainties and doctrines that were religious both in tone and in nature something that any Anglo-Saxon liberal mind like his would find disturbing and even indecent. Such pedagogy, which may be said to somehow represent the peripatetic character of life, appears now but a manifestation—perhaps the dominant—of Cobb's peculiar persona.

It is significant, in this regard, that Cobb's most important contributions to the art of architecture appear now to have all taken place in Boston and that, uncannily, they also appear to coincide, as far as architecture in concerned, with the most important events of the city of Boston at large. Listed chronologically, they are as follows: the Boston Government Centre Master plan (1961), the John Hancock Tower in Copley Square (1966-1975), the new course of the Harvard Graduate School of Design (1980-1985) and finally the recently completed Boston Courthouse (1992-1998)—the most dramatic one being, without doubt, the protracted series of spectacular events that unfolded before and during the construction process of the John Hancock Tower, the one building of the twentieth century about which "more is known than anyone has ever known about any building."

The story's origin are closely connected with Cobb's own. "Origins are a fact, full stop, but nothing to be proud of" used to say Isaiah Berlin, who equated doing so with surrendering to the dubious determinism of blood. Even if somehow proud of his origins, Cobb, a ninth-generation Harvardian, a member of one of the oldest New England families, has never appeared to draw any sense of superiority from them. If anything, he feels somewhat ambivalent, being unsure, I think, of what kind of relationship one should establish with one's own roots—a sentiment somehow reciprocated, curiously, in the very fashions that Bostonians have had towards him throughout his lifetime. Indeed, the way Cobb has been perceived on Boston ground throughout his lifetime ranging from destroyer of the architectural compendium of American architecture to troubler of Boston skyline—must have changed his own understanding of his own roots. This is why it is easy to perceive as an irony of history the very fact that, of all people, Cobb should have been the one responsible for one of the most controversial undertakings ever to take place in Boston after having left the city precisely because he thought that "nothing of interest would happen" around there within his lifetime. The truth of the matter, in fact, is that, in spite of his disinterest in returning to Boston, in a matter of a few years Cobb found himself more involved on Boston ground than any other practicing architect, having become responsible for some of the boldest and most extreme undertakings that characterized one of the most extreme, not to mention extremely fast-paced, "building fever" ever to invest the Boston peninsula in its history. The John Hancock tower in Copley Square was the most extreme case.

Needless to say, the building is today unanimously regarded, at once, as one of the most beautiful high-rises ever put together and as a sort of symbol of Boston and of its "guilty conscience," to put it as Cobb himself put it during one of our conversations. John Updike described it in a short story as "the vertical cousin to the horizontal blue hugeness of the sea," a result of the architect vision of dreaming about an invisible, though immense, building. Ward Just, in an inspired line, saw it as "a Mondrian among Turners" and, more glibly, as "Boston's past reflected in Boston's future." Whatever the metaphor, however, the reflection of sky and of the brick skyline of the Back Bay no doubt remains one of the key aspects of the building, a building which, as is usually customary for great works of architecture, is the outcome of a great number of many struggles—an instance in which almost every single force that is customarily indispensable for producing a significant urban statement by way of a significant work of architecture—namely, power, exhibition of power, client/architect struggle—melted together in the most dramatic way in an urban area that is almost sacred in North America in general and to Bostonians in particular.

Cobb has had a few contacts with conflicting power systems in his life, yet the Hancock case remains the most extreme of such cases and indeed he today does not look forward to the prospect of having such ranking challenged by any other undertaking he might find himself involved with having gone through, throughout the sixties and the seventies, early versions of the scandalistic press coverage that eventually succeeded in mounting an affair of international proportion. A fact that, when the comedy turned into tragedy as the scandal unfolded, rendered Cobb terrified about the many possible interventions that, in the midst of the public outrage, the client wanted to perform on the building in order to "fix" the glass problem. But also a fact that brought Cobb, a Bostonian naturally inclined to understament, as close as one can possibly can to entertaining the prospect of putting an end to his career.

Cobb seems to have retained from such contacts a profound understanding of a little talked-about, yet fundamental problem that architects must face: namely the need to understand how conflicting power systems interact with each other and more importantly how the architect should interact with and indeed make the most out of them in order to attempt to ameliorate urban life—an understanding that now appears to be one of the most developed muscles of Cobb's vigilant brain. Ethical questions and entrepreneurship are, I think, the others—three atoms that define the monad of heartfelt loyalties that defines his career.

The point is that Hancock-like undertakings have convinced him that the underlying thesis of his Harvard education—namely that to all genuine questions there had to be one and one only true answer, all the other answers being false—makes in fact little sense, being nothing more than an attempt to escape from the unpredictability of life to land in the false security of fairy tales. Indeed, his career makes him feel today that general propositions, their relation to truth and falsehood, knowledge and opinion and the impossibility of verifying the proposition they express are meaningless when confronted with empirical problems, namely the problems that he as an architect is, and always was, interested in solving. His thesis today is that concrete situations never follow theoretical constructs and, furthermore, that what in theory may appear to be unacceptable may in actuality turn not out to be so; or it may even turn out, paradoxically, to be desirable. His exercises in the tall office building field-one of the major fields of his career—compounded this lesson by teaching him not only that no two situations are alike and strategies that work in one place could hardly work in a different one, but also that situations which, in principle present themselves in general terms as the reverse of promising may, in real life, reserve the most unexpected aesthetic pleasures—the John Hancock Tower being a case in point.

Of course, there is no definitive way to know exactly when these ideas took shape in his mind; yet, having spent two years in thinking about this, I have recently come to the conclusion that his own "theoretical construct," even if as removed as possible from systematic pretensions, began to organize itself in Cobb's mind at the time when he assumed his chairmanship at the Harvard GSD a few years after the

John Hancock experience had been completed—an office that, in retrospect, might have come to him through such an experience. This is why one may think that, uncannily, Cobb's whole intellectual life had been a reckoning with "Harvard experiments," which is to say with experiments that were generated at Harvard and had somehow unprecedented consequences upon his psyche. In the forties, when his generation was intoxicated with doctrinarism, Cobb questioned many aspects of it, being suspicious of Gropius's elusiveness and ungratefulness in his own compositional capacities. In the eighties, when, alone in his class, he assumed the very office that Gropius held, he used all the elements in his power to put forward the idea that the search for doctrinaire, all-embracing belief systems, should be regarded as a sure sign of dogmatism—something that, being himself somewhat allergic to it, he could only find inappropriate, if not misleading for students.

An attitude reflected in his teaching style, which he tried to fulfil by participating to as many reviews as possible and in meeting frequently with students. "Well, you know, you always try to compensate for the wrongs done to you and to me was that Walter Gropius did not participate in the school at all, except for his dozen master students. He never came to reviews. He never attended anything. He gave some lectures but he never gave courses. He paid attention only to his master thesis students, a small group. That did not seem right to me. So I tried to participate to every studio review, which I pretty much did."

In September 1980, when the first event of his tenure, a lecture by John Hejduck, was misunderstood by students who appeared more conclusive than he was, he was left mixed feelings about the generation gap. Gradually, though, the fact that the student body seemed baffled by the idea that "architecture may lend itself to acknowledge a problem and not necessarily to solve it" began to intrigue him because, for him, this was the very fact that made life worth living. Nowhere else is Cobb's attitude more evident than in the two lectures that frame his tenure at the GSD and that, in however partial a form, also frame the pedagogical program that he helped to put forward at Harvard.

In his first, aptly titled "Where I Stand," he was able to define where he stood in relation to the school. He introduced himself and talked much about the "great many questions" that were burdening his mind and very little about preconceived answers.

He put forward four fixed attitudes—coherence, rigor, openness and audacity—that, in his eyes, formed the four cardinal points that should lead the school out of its doldrums.

In 1985, after a five-year long period in which the school had been invested by the above attitudes, he concluded his term as a chairman by delivering a lecture called "Architecture and the University" at Sanders Theatre. There, for the first time, a well thought-out attempt to take issue with one of the central dilemmas of architecture schools was offered to architectural audiences: "Of what use architecture may be to the University?" and conversely, "Of what use the University may be to architecture?" is what he asked the Harvard audience. That both constituencies may be of some use to each other instead of being in conflict with each other was his message.

A meditation about the power resident within an institution like Harvard University as cast by its role of introducing a certain idea of modernism in America, "Architecture and the University" has become the most thoughtful statement delivered in the recent past about the mutual benefit that a school of architecture and a university can have on each other. In it Cobb sharply distinguished his side from the radical and somewhat fanatic credo of his "teacher" by expressing his unwillingness to take any side at all. His point is that both constituencies could only embrace the "acute cultural ambivalence" of the contemporary era.

Speaking from the very same chair from which Gropius spoke some four decades earlier, Cobb set out to demonstrate how the pedagogy he had in mind, in order to be useful, had to be contrary in nature to the set of moralistic instructions that his generation had to come to terms with: no single truth, no Ptolemaic systems, indeed no belief system whatsoever: instead, the sponsorship of a critical discourse about architecture which, in turn, should be "thought of and practiced as a radical critique of the culture—a critique carried out in the language of forms rather than the language of words."

About all the assumptions of his Harvard education, Cobb feels today as he has felt for a long time, namely that he himself has little to say. Or to do. If society were different from what it is, perhaps it would be possible to conceive utopian urban visions, Ville Radieuse-like, like the ones that filled his student days. But it is clear that this is not so, nor can't be so. Above all, he is clear that society, in that event, would have to differ too greatly from society as it is, or society as it always has been. He therefore finds it unnecessary to discuss the prospect of what cannot be, even in principle, part of human affairs. What ought to be done must be defined in practicable rather than in imaginary terms. This is why he understands utopian urban visions as conceptually incoherent, given their predisposition to present themselves as the solution to all the evils of cities. Architecture is what it is—just architecture: a physical, immediate thing that certainly cannot be called upon or used for curing all the troubles of society. It is a shell for human purposes, if you want, and not much more. To advocate abstract, ideal measures, suitable for all conditions, as the second generation of Modern/ist architects seem, in retrospect, too often to have done, appears to him now visionary, irresponsible, and somehow leading to oversimplification or even to dangerous speculations.

Today, some two decades later, Cobb is still adamant about this, having his entire career ready to prove, if necessary, his belief, the latter being somehow straightened, I maintain, by his early exposure to the much-advertised splendour of a seemingly unbreakable rock, the rock of the *neue sachlichkeit*, whose conception of objective artistic value as a result of objective artistic behaviours was at the root of the excitement of many members of his generation, to repeat, the third generation of Modern/ist architects. It is this rock of unifying monistic beliefs generating unifying monistic patterns, which is at the very heart of modernistic credo that Cobb seems, in effect, to have split open both in his psyche and his buildings. To say this is not to say that so great a reversal is due, or can be due, to his individual acts. Many besides him, like the Venturis, no doubt, supplied the dynamite. My only purpose is to acknowledge that, among all of those who challenged Modernist ethics rather than modern forms, Cobb is one who has carried his challenge a long way ahead by establishing an open school model that appears now an achievement of the first order—indeed, one of the major items of Cobb's intellectual estate and thanks to which in part the cultural atmosphere of the American academia of the present day is equipped with less moralism, less religion and no prevailing style.

Cobb, of course, will never claim that he had embraced

pluralism in a conscious way. "I certainly did not have any explicit intention of embracing pluralism" was his response when pressed to say what his intellectual agenda had been or to explain why he invited so many contesting parties at the same time. This strategy of self-concealment would lead him to add that his actions were but a mere reflection of other movements developing in the culture at large. His main goal, as far as he is concerned, was to "reconnect the school to the profession" in North America—since, for him, after 1968 and its aftermath, "nothing less than the discipline of architecture was at stake."

While, no doubt, this is true, it remains that Harvard seems to be the place where Cobb found himself after having spent half a lifetime in coming to terms with his own education. It was at Harvard, in fact, that Cobb, some thirty years after his graduation found the "one big thing" that he was looking for in his student days and that was to order his intellectual life thereafter: a defence of pluralism which insisted on the impossibility of reconciling all ends of building activities or, for that matter, all ends of human affairs. This defence was one that would ultimately take the form of exposing the student body to the entire spectrum of architectural speculation evolving at the time, which meant anxiety, discomfort, destabilization, very many heated debates—in a word, the feeling of what it means to be an architect. This defence meant, in other words, exposing the student body to what were, and still are, in his experience "the essential preconditions to the production of architecture," namely "a correct understanding of the anomalies, inconsistencies and contradictions that are likely to be found in any institutional building program."

At Harvard Cobb performed as an educator *sui generis* and certainly his short "academic career" is worth-thinking about, as Cobb had certainly never expected, or intended to be, a leader of architectural thought of any sort. He had published very little and never developed an interest in organizing his writings—mostly remarks, notes, introductions, thoughts—in a collected form. In fact he is the least academic of all the academics in architecture, the range of his interests bursting through all the usual restraints and cautions of academic circles.

"I believe in the rotation of leadership. I think that the academic world is overburdened by this kind of lifetime commitment. People who have to live with each other for a lifetime and build defensive positions. You just have to shake it up. And I think that the idea of rotating chairmanship is a good idea," is a typical comment about the academic world on his part.

"I am not like most people who live in the academic world for whom time is a very secondary consideration. Universities move slowly. I never intended to spend more than five years as a chairman, not so much because I did not want to or could not, but because I thought that rotation is in fact a very good thing in that position. I felt that I had to move fast and decisively," another. Taken together, these remarks make me think that it must be a matter of amusement to him that his "notorious" profligacy in giving his time to the great number of students who consulted him is still a topic of discussion at the Harvard GSD. To them, somebody who does not want to go on the record told me, it seemed as if he had retained all of their words and, in turn, returned them back—the words—enriched by his genuine and dispassionate views regardless of either the topic or the point they—the students—were trying to make. A performance delivered without any sense of delivering a performance but, instead, with a deeply felt sense of transferring experience. A comment to which I can only add my own experience of speaking with Henry Cobb, the hour-long answers that he would offer in reply to many of the questions that I put before him, often making connections between disparate topics in disparate fashions but in one, unmistakable tone of voice—one which is the joy of transcribers and typists alike but also one that accounts for his own way of being an architect.

Of his most recently completed project, the Boston Courthouse, Cobb said once to me once during one of our conversations, that "it has simply proved that talking is more difficult that remaining silent. When you talk you have to be saying something and speaking in a certain tone of voice. It is not only what you say but how you say it. When you remain silent it is much easier to be poetic." Since this remark was made in a particularly slow fashion, the sense of his out loud reasoning, struggling through the issue became to me more apparent than usual. I said at the outset that his fashion of speaking may important to understand the man and his intelligence, which is anything but inarticulate.

What I meant by that is that while most of us need to struggle across the gulf existing between our words and our thought, Cobb's mind seems to operate in a different fashion, his intelligence being so articulate that his words are but the materialization of his thoughts. His words and thoughts, in fact, lead each other on, as if they were complementary yet indispensable agents of the very same aesthetic phenomenon, one that retains everything and forgets nothing, as one of his most deeply felt formula—one which summarizes, to conclude, the man and the architect, his voice and his acute mind—has it: "No voice should ever be allowed to be heard without its counter voice."

The American Architect as an Entrepreneur

a note

Published in west workroom, Milan: Charta, 2007

This piece reflects the sheer enthusiasm generated by a figure like Zeckendorf, a figure who has largely vanished from the contemporary scene, as its politically correctness rhetoric would make it impossible for people like him to operate. It is a status that may arguably explain why undertakings requiring unfettered optimism like building the United Nations' headquarters in Midtown Manhattan are quite inconceivable, if not ostracized, today.

'Pei's partner and one-time student, Henry Cobb, was to be the architect in charge of our Canadian venture. I suspected that a New England Yankee might get along well in old Montreal, and twenty-nine-year-old Henry, a bright, very talented, and most circumspect young man, was the scion of an old Boston family. [...] Soon after our first New York meeting with Gordon [president of the Canadian National Railways], Cobb and I flew up to confer at the site. The 'hole' Gordon wanted to fill was just north of the railroad station, the principal department stores, and St. James Street financial area. A great, new building complex, a sort of Rockefeller Center-cum-Grand Central Station, could create a new center of gravity and focal point for the city. This location would provide the 'centricity' which Montreal needed, to make the project click. I was enthusiastic, made no bones about letting the CNR know how we felt, and gladly committed Webb & Knapp to the $250,000 it would take to draw comprehensive plans. [...] By late winter and early spring of 1956, Cobb was ready with preliminary plans for Montreal. He and Vince Ponte, our city planner, as well as some Look magazine people who were doing a story on Webb & Knapp, flew to Montreal with me in our DC-3. Circling the city at a few thousand feet, I looked over the site while studying Cobb's design.

Because we were concerned about the conservative atmosphere that pervaded Montreal, Cobb had prepared a step-by-step design. On an elevated platform plaza over the "hole," he set two rectangular towers plus a number of lower, subsidiary buildings. In this way, only after the first tower was successful would we need to put money down for the second structure. It was a competent and pleasant design, but as I stood up in the steeply banked airplane, and looked out of the windows to the winter-gripped city below, I was dissatisfied. Something was missing. Here lay this unexploited but potentially fabulous site which only we could develop, but what we proposed to develop lacked power. As I began to sense what was missing, I said, "Harry, I want to tell you something...you do not make 'melly' out of a blue white diamond."

The minute I explained that "melly" are merely the bits and chips left over when a great diamond has been cut, he saw what I meant. He, too, recognized that we needed something with enough critical mass to force changes on Montreal. By critical mass I mean not only the physical but also the emotional and the aesthetic impact on a truly successful building complex. We then and there set out the final specifications, within which Cobb was free to design as his genius dictated. I told him we wanted a major building of at least 1.5 million square feet total area, with at least 35,000 square feet per floor. It must be designed to provide corporate identity for more than one major tenant. Given these directions, Cobb went off to produce the plans of the great cruciform building that now so powerfully dominates downtown Montreal. This was the design that I took to Gordon. What we determined on that airplane was the most crucial decision of the whole Montreal project.'[1]

This powerful, beautiful, revelatory and strangely overlooked passage was written (in his autobiography) by William Zeckendorf. Little talked about, if at all, today, Zeckendorf was, still is, a man of great significance for the discipline of architecture—one who, uncannily, is to

1. William Zeckendorf, *William Zeckendorf* (Canada: Holt, Rinehart and Winston, 1970) pp. 170, 171.

this day neither fully acknowledged nor understood inside the scholarly world, to say nothing of the pseudo-scholarly world. His importance is counterbalanced by fairly widespread incomprehension of the exact nature of his thinking and actions-a misunderstanding that in turn results from a lack of familiarity with Zeckendorf's own goals and with their aims at securing a firm foundation for the practice of architecture in the twentieth century. Too vast to be put in a nutshell, Zeckendorf appears to be a case of a single body housing multiple ideas and personalities. Many ways are available to describe him. He could be portrayed as the one who, having suggested that the United Nations Headquarters might sit well on the six-block long area facing the East River in Midtown Manhattan-an area that he owned and that was eventually donated to the UN by John D. Rockefeller, Jr. who purchased it from him-made New York "the capital of the world" by a single stroke of pure genius while having breakfast on December 6, 1946. He could also be portrayed as the first man who had car-telephones. Arguably Bell Atlantic's most important client, Zeckendorf is one of the first individuals who developed an addictive attachment to the telephone receiver, a device he relied on to air the many sounds of his voice. Whatever the judgment, Zeckendorf remains a magnetic man by any standard and he certainly functioned as such—a magnet—to two architects, namely I. M. Pei and Henry N. Cobb, turning upside down the general understanding of an architect's usual career in a modern, I daresay American, fashion. In summary, and more to the point, Zeckendorf can here be introduced as the founder of that most interesting "planning agency" which most contributed to shaping the concept of the American architect as an entrepreneur—a figure almost unknown before the Second

World War and still very little known outside of the Unites States. It is the purpose of this paper to begin to fulfill the need of an analysis of such a figure.

To begin at the beginning, I feel compelled to notice how most observers of the American scene have consistently failed to see the magnetic power of the man-a power that, from the very first time I heard of him, exercised a great fascination over me as I was in the process of helping Cobb to deliver his intimate thoughts about his firm, his career and his architecture, all of which will soon be celebrated in a long-overdue monograph. This is why I once induced Cobb to give me his first-hand impressions of Zeckendorf. It was on November 11, 1996, and we had started to have a conversation about irony in architecture. The page devoted to that day in my journal goes as follows.

"A conversation on irony. Cobb: 'I. M. Pei is the least ironic person I have ever met. This characteristic is reflected in the character of his work. I am not ironic either. This is what we shared. James Freed is a little bit more ironic than we are.' He then added that Pei was not comfortable in the States until he got to Boston. At first I did not see his point. Cobb made it clear to me. He said that this was not so much because of Boston's traditional trade with China, but rather because of the hospitality and the value system of New England. The thought of the importance of this to architecture crossed my mind, but I did not dare to mention it. Cobb did so shortly thereafter. He then nonchalantly said that, looking at his career, one could perceive a twist. He said that, in recent work especially, he has become a different architect, having embraced, almost unconsciously, Vico's doctrine of incompatible truths. Architecture can do that. Not just the mind. This led us to talk about Venturi and his way of being ironic. 'In a way,' Cobb said,

'I disagree with Venturi.' Cobb made it clear that Venturi's irony is still about a belief system. 'It is a critique of it. That is his *métier*.' I said he was very good at it. Cobb nodded his head. Having entered a stream-of-consciousness mood, Cobb turned to some acquaintances of his, a couple of Gropius loyalists who acquired the belief system in the forties and never quite recovered from it.

Their main purpose was—and still is—to make a movie of modern architecture. A movie full of Heroes and Villains. The latter being the so-called murderers of Modern Architecture, namely Venturi and Philip Johnson. Or Arthur Drexler. He finally returned to his own predicament and his own way out. Here Cobb said that, not being equipped with Venturi's irony, he adopted the notion that the architect can and must be ready to acknowledge that contradictory truths can in fact coexist. He himself acknowledged that such a mental posture is what decisively separated his late work from his early work. Here I brought up the case of the Hancock Tower in Boston. Cobb spoke of it as the hinge of his life. The Hancock Tower acknowledged a contradiction, an inconsistency, whatever one wants to call it, Cobb said.

This was also the hinge on which the conversation turned. From irony we moved to audacity, namely Zeckendorf's own audacity and capacity to live in several different worlds simultaneously. The topic, it is true, was introduced by me. I could not resist having a first-hand description of Zeckendorf. Cobb spoke of him using sentences that arose from some of my remarks:' Zeckendorf had very large appetites in every sense. He was big in lots of ways. He liked to live well. He had a very good and large [wine] cellar.... Most of all, he had the capacity to transcend the field in which he was operating. The real estate world is brutal and crass. It is not a world for you and me. He mastered that world. At the same time he lived in the world of Rockefeller, MoMA, architecture.... A world of money, if you want, but money was to him an instrument; he was not a good manager, but a great entrepreneur. Most people who succeed in real estate are very smart but not very imaginative. Zeckendorf was equipped with both of those qualities. The word unique is overused in a terrible way, but Zeckendorf was a unique person. What separates him from other developers is that, instead of keeping us in the dark, instead of adopting the notorious mushroom management, he wanted us to know what was going on. He always told us what we needed to know and not what we did not need to know. His interest in architecture was in using it to make a better space to live in. Most clients do not tell you what they should be telling you, and tell you lots of things that they should not be telling you. Zeckendorf was the opposite. On top of that, William Zeckendorf was also a man of large visions. Those visions were sometimes larger than his own capacity.' The idealism embedded in Zeckendorf persona was, at this point, very clear. Cobb said that William Zeckendorf could be called a dreamer. I replied to this by observing Zeckendorf's astonishing capacity to implement his own dreams. This brought us to Vico's other theory: the idea that one understands only what one does. In this light, William Zeckendorf becomes a very pragmatic dreamer. Cobb confirmed that to be the case. He knew how to seize the opportunity, Cobb said.

This, added to the opening paragraphs of this paper, should be sufficient to give the reader a taste of Zeckendorf's persona. To explore some of the central concerns of William Zeckendorf as a developer-if one can confine so vast a man in so cramped a category-should be my next duty, as these are concerns which, from a somewhat different perspective, but no less cramped a category, Cobb shared with Zeckendorf, while learning from him.

If Zeckendorf was obsessed with anything it was with the relation of quality to the city, and so was Cobb. Zeckendorf came at this issue from the side of real estate, Cobb from the side of architecture. Two disparate sides, one can argue. Yet, it is indisputable that the opening quotation portrays a conjunction-one where, in all frankness, I think the two men met. The quotation, in fact, portrays much more than their professional relationship: it shows a fortunate conjunction of men with individual yet imaginative, visions—a conjunction which was necessary to the implementation of as vast an urban undertaking as PVM-Place Ville Marie in Montreal which can be said to be Cobb's significant *opera prima* at an urban scale.

The analysis of the merits of that particular undertaking is undoubtedly beyond the scope of the present article, which is just trying to bring into focus the fact that, in 1950, Cobb moved to New York City to join I. M. Pei, who had just established an architectural division sponsored by Webb & Knapp, the real estate agency run by Zeckendorf. A decision individually taken, of course. Yet, since any particular decision brings out certain aspects of a general condition—Why was an architect attracted at all to a real estate developer?—it should be noticed that this particular move dramatized certain issues and muted others. What is brought to immediate notice by this decision of Cobb is the striking difference between New York and Boston at a general level and, at a more specific level, between the "planning strategies" of Zeckendorf's architectural task force and a Gropius-centered Harvard Graduate School of Design.

In retrospect, it seems indeed grotesque that no historians writing histories of architecture in America in the second half of the twentieth century have devoted any pages to William Zeckendorf while, in turn, so much emphasis had been put on the so-called Gropius legacy. What is even more striking is that to associate oneself with Zeckendorf was, at that time, considered unethical and naughty by the so-called *commonauté des clercs* who gathered around Gropius's persona and who, not unexpectedly, did not waste time in judging it professionally unacceptable.

It would be vain, given the vastness of the topic, to attempt to establish here a scientific comparison between Boston and New York. Yet it is perhaps safe to see both Gropius and Zeckendorf as representing the essence of interesting events happening in both places. When I asked Cobb about this, on August 4, 1997, we had the following conversation.

"Nothing in my training at the GSD prepared me for Zeckendorf. One thing is clear: I wanted to be involved in big things. My original assumption was that, in order to do that, one had to deal with socialism. The idea of the new architecture and the new society. In Boston there was no new architecture and no new society. In New York, a trace of both was easily perceivable. The thing about New York is its instability. Boston is fixed. New York is open. New York is about bigness and openness. These are still the two things about New York. It is also an addiction. If you are addicted to bigness and openness, you have to be in New York. It is not a quality judgment. In a sense it was the available alternative to socialism. Had I been English, I would have gone to design New Towns. I would have loved that. And I actually thought about it. My early aspirations was certainly connected with urbanism, with architecture serving society and making a better world. In a way, it is very hard for me to separate the way I felt about New York from the way I felt about Zeckendorf. I felt as if I were in touch with the essence of New York. He was quintessential New York. I felt I was in touch with the most exciting aspects of New York, at least as far as architecture is concerned."

"Which is not exactly the way the other architects felt!" I said.

His reply: "Not at all. I think it was against professional ethics to practice architecture in association with a developer. The AIA was very unhappy about it. I do not recall all the details, but the substance of it was that it was considered unprofessional. It was not a good thing to do. Especially not a good thing for people with the kind of aspirations that we had. They said that we were thumbing our nose at the profession, and, of course, we did. In a way we were not interested in the profession, but, rather, in doing things."

"How was a real estate developer perceived at the time?"

"I'd say that there were two kinds of real estate developer, brokers and the low-end people. People who built white brick houses. Zeckendorf did not fit into either category. And I'd never have been interested in working for a real estate developer other than Zeckendorf."

"Did anybody from the architectural side ever perceive his essential role in bringing the UN headquarters to New York?"

"The UN role was perceived, but people tended to forget it. Zeckendorf was never considered a great citizen. He was too unconventional. He was not accepted by the establishment. The business community did business and went along with him but, in the end, nobody stepped in to help him when he was in trouble. He was a very engaging man to work with, and he did create a lot of opportunity for us."

What, at this juncture, I think is worth reporting is the fact that, even if for a limited number of individuals, and even if not officially recognized in this capacity, Webb &

Knapp's architectural division turned out to be a whole university in its own right. Recalling that time during an office talk in June 1968, Cobb stated unambiguously: "We learned an enormous amount from Mr. Zeckendorf. In fact, I think all of us who participated in those ten years would agree now, and probably would still agree ten years from now, that it is the most important formative experience as professionals that we had. [...] All of these projects that we did during those years had one thing in common which really has virtually gone out of practice today, and that is that they were all speculative in nature, that is to say that there were not designed as a result of a great corporation or an institution deciding that they need to have certain amount of space in a certain place and coming to us to design a building, rather they were the result of William Zeckendorf's entrepreneurial initiative to find a piece of property which he felt had a certain potential and then ask us as architects and planners to extract from that particular situation the maximum we could in terms of attractiveness of the buildings and spaces to the users that we wanted to bring into the project. So that it is a completely different kind of enterprise. It calls for a rather special kind of partnership between the client and the architect-planner."

A synthesis. A summing up. Something to help the reader to understand the peculiarity of this powerful association within the scenario of American architecture. I can best do this reporting a few thoughts that Cobb delivered to me on May 17, 1997, when I told him that I was under the impression that the Adelphi Terrace by Robert Adams had to be included among his passions. Cobb's extended reply was as follows.

"The Adelphi Terrace belongs, indeed, to that group. It embodies a historical interest which kind of reflects the

Zeckendorf period. At a certain moment I became very interested in the history of cities prompted by Place Ville Marie. I became very interested in the notion that building in cities has to be thought of as an operation on a living organism and not as just putting another object into a fixed entity. I became very interested in the way that cities are transformed as they develop, and the kinds of initiatives that lie behind these transformations. Because of my experience with Zeckendorf, I became particularly interested in what I perceive to be a missing sense in most histories of cities: the sense of enterprise. What I mean is this: most urban history talks about form and talks about the way cities are shaped by political policy, by kings or popes or whatever, but there is very little attention given to the way that cities have been shaped by speculative enterprise. I became very interested in that, because I had experienced the way cities could be shaped by speculative enterprise. What I perceived was that there was a lacuna in the historical treatment of cities that resulted from an insensitivity or lack of understanding of certain motivations that are very active in the city that have to do with speculative enterprise." I responded: "What exactly do you mean by speculative enterprise?" His reply: "By speculative enterprise I mean building projects that are driven by the desire to seize the opportunity presented by certain circumstances in the city, the opportunity to envision transformations in the city, but I became particularly interested in London in general and Adam in particular.

For example, Covent Garden was an interesting example of speculative development, and London, in fact, is the city in which, in a historical sense, you can study speculative development. But the truth is that London, as you know, was from its origin protected from the dictates of the monarchy. It was a city that the King actually had to ask permission to enter; therefore it was not like Rome and Paris, a city which became the plaything of the monarch, but it did become the plaything of large landowners and nobility, some of whom were extraordinarily sensitive to the potential for profit in their holdings through an imaginative understanding of the way cities work."

"An area in which Zeckendorf excelled, I take it."

"Absolutely. And, in fact, this is the connection between my experience with Zeckendorf and history. I can give you a very simple example which brings me to the Adelphi. As you well know, the genius of Zeckendorf was exemplified by his understanding that although the land fronting on the East River between 42nd and 50th streets in New York had become essentially an industrial slum of slaughterhouses and that, in fact, it had lost all its value as land—like the frontage on First Avenue—nonetheless, it was not prevented from becoming an object of speculative enterprise. I told you before that Zeckendorf knew how to seize opportunity.

I should here add that he also had this capacity to imagine how you could transform the city if you could deal with an area like the slaughterhouses in a comprehensive way and that, by doing that, one could in fact do something which is one of the vivid lessons I learned from Zeckendorf, which he didn't call it anything because he wasn't interested in theorizing but I would call 'reversal of frontage' which I have found to be an extraordinarily important thing to understand.

The idea is that if you can take what is perceived to be a back door and turn it into a front door, you are playing a whole new game and possibilities that were unimaginable suddenly become real. The slaughterhouses, of course, are an example, of making the river an asset by turning everything around. Adelphi Terrace was, in my view, probably the most vivid example of what I would call "multiple reversals of frontage" over a period of centuries.

Adelphi Terrace is the paradigmatic case of a lot of things that I'm interested in—the way that cities are always changing, nothing is fixed, the phenomenon of reversal of frontage, the phenomenon of the intervention of an imaginative risk-taking enterprise in a situation which most people don't see, but the entrepreneur sees it. But also the encountering of many difficulties."

I sat thinking. After a small pause I learned that Henry James had expressed something similar to this in the following fashion: "A great building is the greatest conceivable work of art, because it represents difficulties annulled, resources combined, labor, courage and patience."

What Cobb retains from this idea—that the professionalization of the role of the architect as it has unfolded in America over the now closing century is a field of study of primary importance-is something that, I would argue, would have pleased Giambattista Vico, the first (philosopher) to have formulated the idea of cultures as entities which are essentially different from one another.

What this means is that what mattered to a fifth-century Greek is very different from matters to a native American or, for that matter, to a twentieth century New England Yankee, to circle back to William Zeckendorf's own portray of Cobb. Perhaps a confirmation of the centrality of entrepeneurial skills, which I have tried to illustrate here, to American architecture in general and to the unprecedented figure of the American architect, as it has defined itself in the second half of the twentieth century, in particular.

A Harvard educator as an impresario

Berlin, 2016. Unpublished

The following piece intends to recall the now overlooked job performed by Cobb as chairman at the Harvard GSD which can be said to simultaneously embody a mirror image of Walter Gropius' performance four decades prior, and the role carried out by the second-to-last dean (would-be chairman) three decades later. The piece also provides untarnished and genuine material for the not often underplayed (if not rejected) discontents about the role of a profession like architecture within academic settings. The piece is an edited version of a talk I gave at the Berlin branch of Northeastern University in 2015.

'The problem with the pedagogy in place at the GSD in the 1940s under Gropius was that, while it was based on the idea that architecture was now liberated from the tyranny of dead styles there was alarmingly little substance or coherence. There was, in my view, an absence of the kind of discipline that is the traditional precursor of achieving mastery of in any field. In other words, there was no coherent program of training.

There were ideas about it, based, in Gropius's mind, on the Bauhaus program of so-called basic design, and was about acquiring what I would call eye-hand skills related to drawing and modeling and composition, things of this kind, but I don't recall it as a coherent series of exercises and, of course, there was no Kandinsky, Klee, Breuer, Moholy Nagy, or Albers in sight. I recall it as being weak, both in concept and in execution. I did not have the skill or the innate ability to overcome that weakness and that's why, for me, it was a void. For more gifted students, it might not have been such a void, because they had it in their fingers, they brought their fingers with them to the school, they brought that capacity with them. There was no discipline.

We didn't have to draw bricks for a year, the way that the student at IIT did, but there was another kind of tyranny, which was the tyranny of proscription. That is to say, history was proscribed. In a way, that kind of tyranny, the kind of tyranny that compels you to remain ignorant, is the worst kind of tyranny. The tyranny of the Mies school was a tyranny of a training, a kind of discipline that you were obliged to undergo but, the assumption of the Mies school was that those who are gifted, having absorbed this discipline and training, will then use it as a base from which to invent their own architecture and those who are less gifted will at least do less harm, because they will work within a discipline.

That's the same premise as the Ecole des Beaux-Arts or as any training program. At Harvard, that was missing.

I would say that the Mies school and the Gropius school represented two flawed programs but, those who graduated from the Mies school, like my partner Ingo Freed, spent half a lifetime trying to escape from the prison in which they felt themselves enclosed by the Miesian discipline and the Miesian ideology. Those who went to the Gropius school, on the other hand, like myself, spent an equal amount of time trying to discover something worth believing in because, certainly at the GSD, we didn't learn anything worth believing in. The belief system was a social program, and that's fine, but, in the end, architecture is about form, and the formal program was simply absent. There was a disjunction, there was the absence of everything that one might learn from history and nothing took its place. So, again, this could explain—in my case, it does explain—why I was looking for a certain discipline which I did not have. First of all, I would not find it in history, because I didn't know enough history. Yet, I was ideologically committed to a new architecture. But how would I find a new architecture?'

These are the words used by Henry Nichols Cobb to describe the Harvard Design School he attended as a student (MArch I program) from 1946-49. Like many fellow students, he had become attracted to the idea of becoming an architect by falling victim to a spell that was generated by a rather unique set of European events with great consequences in America, since the country provided shelter for a number of German architects who had been forced to escape the Nazi regime that closed down the industrial design school (with unfulfilled architecture aspirations) they were associated with called the Bauhaus. The forced closure and consequent exile status cast on its more prominent faculty members, in turn, gave a mythological status to its brand. This was true for the American audience more than for others. Though unlike many of his other fellow students, Cobb joined the academic program equipped with quite unusual ties to the Institution. If the expression Harvard-born-and-bred has any meaning, Cobb can be considered a poster boy for it. The first member of his family had enrolled at Harvard College in 1799. The family tradition continued for nine consecutive generations and, like almost all of his family's predecessors, he was also a graduate of Harvard College when he entered the school.[1]

---

1. People with limited knowledge of the American setting are unaware of the fact that Harvard College and Harvard University are two separate academic settings hosted under one umbrella. The first, devoted to undergraduates, is the original Harvard School, (founded in 1636 and named after the clergyman, John Harvard) and it stands as the oldest institution of higher learning in the United States. The second is the umbrella covering ten professional schools designed to prepare people to enter a chosen profession. It was conceived as such by President Charles William Eliot who transformed the college and affiliated professional schools into a modern research university in 1900. What even fewer people are aware of is that the institution is governed by two entities: the Harvard Corporation and the Board of Overseers. Therefore, Harvard also stands as the oldest corporation in the USA. Probably originally intended to be a body of the school's resident instructors, similar to the fellows of an Oxbridge college, it quickly turned into the now-familiar American model of a governing board—an outside body whose members are not involved in the institution's daily life. It meets periodically to consult with the day-to-day head, the president (whom it appoints).

The Corporation is self-perpetuating, appointing new members to fill its own vacancies as they arise, and stands like a pre-modern, impenetrable body of power which is different from market-based corporations,. For most of its history, the Corporation consisted of six fellows in addition to the president. But the unacceptable, large endowment decline (10 billion dollars, or 25% of the total) that happened in 2008 forced Harvard to announce in 2010 that the

If he had one obsession upon graduation (1949), it was to leave the Harvard campus and the urban area of Boston, because he perceived it as still dwelling in the XIX century. He wanted to immerse himself in the *spirit of the time* that appeared to be 'wired' in the air a few hundred miles south in New York City. At the time, he could not possibly ever imagine in his wildest dreams that, decades later, life circumstances would lead him to take on the same role Gropius had during his own time as a student: to chair the architecture department, with an uncannily similar agenda: get architecture education in 'some sort of shape.'

A quick historical outline is germane here given the particular role played by the Harvard Design School in American education which gave substance to the widely spread belief that Harvard should be considered the *primus inter pares* among equals, a sentiment definitely shared by the members of the Harvard community. This notwithstanding, it remains that whatever is thought about the Hudnut/Gropius era (1937-1952), it is beyond dispute that it did embody an idea that looked very important for a while, namely that the university should and could not only serve to educate people, but also shape the profession by the way it trained architects. This to say that there had been a consciously active intervention on the part of the University by creating the GSD and having a dean (Hudnut) bring Gropius in as chairman of the architecture department and everything

---

Corporation's structure and practices were to be significantly altered: the number of fellows increased from seven to thirteen (with prescribed terms of service) and several new committees would endeavor to improve the group's integration with the activities of the University as a whole, especially its long-term planning.

that ensued. It was a very powerful affirmation of the role of the University, asserting its responsibility and authority, to help shape the field and not just train people for practice.[2]

Gropius was followed by José Luis Sert, the Spanish architect who extended Harvard's leadership through the establishment of the urban design program and urban design conferences. Even more importantly, he performed his activity as an architect and brought architecture very strongly into the consciousness of the University by creating buildings there. Owing to the patronage of University President Pusey, he was able to construct a remarkable number of 'Centers'—Holyoke Centre (1958-65), The Harvard Science Centre (1969-72), the Centre for the Study of World Religion at the Divinity School—and a student housing complex on the river called Peabody Terrace (1962-64). Thus Sert extended the idea of the leadership of both the University and, more importantly, the School to an international level. It therefore can be said that Harvard had asserted itself as being a local institution embraced by an international constituency of students for four decades.

This status came to a screeching halt at the end of the 1960s when Sert retired. A leadership vacuum ensued that lasted for about a decade while a cultural revolution

2. This remains true in spite of the fact that, as a witness like Cobb confirmed, the two men stopped speaking to each other somewhere in the mid-1940s due to their different stances on the relationship that students had to have regarding history. Apparently Hudnut thought that it was fine not to teach a history class because the students, being graduate students, were supposed to be knowledgeable about history. However, Gropius thought that historical precedents should not be talked about, f mentioned at all. So when Hudnut realized the extent of his gullibility, he gct pissed and stopped talking to Gropius, and the results are well-known.

was unfolding. Although it created excitement in many fields, the revolution proved fruitless, if not outright detrimental, for education in the design field. It essentially destroyed the schools of architecture. The GSD was at the centre of the student revolt, which involved not only students, but also faculty. The problem that architecture was having in culture was compounded by the fact that it was perceived as a wild card in the university.[3] Cobb was no stranger to all of the above and knew exactly what he was getting into when he accepted the challenge of the chairmanship. He intended to restore the role of the school in a position of both national and international leadership. He firmly believed that if architecture was going to have a presence in the university, it could only do so if it was perceived as producing culture.

Even though he has always claimed that he did not seek out the job, he stated that he was approached, on the contrary, because he was a well-respected practicing architect (which indeed he was, being a partner of the architect selected by the Kennedy family to design the Kennedy Library in Boston), there is reason to believe that the real story behind the appointment which can be picked up on the street contains a certain degree of (a different) truth, one that links his appointment to the John Hancock tower affair.[4]

---

3. This explains the otherwise incomprehensible anomaly of having a University President (Pusey) appointing a professor of business as dean of the GSD. It shows how Pusey did not feel that he could entrust the school to anyone from the design field.

4. For the reader who is unaware of the controversy, refer to conrad-bercah, bad client/good citizen, notes on Harry Cobb's Hancock Place in, san rocco 12, Spring 2016, which is republished in the present anthology.

As one can imagine, the appointment created quite a stir in the muddy waters of academia, resulting as offensive to a significant number of the tenured faculty members. After all, the appointed 'educator' did not have much teaching experience to speak of and no claim whatsoever to any kind of scholarship or theoretical stance. If anything, he was considered (at least by the most unfair critics) to be a power-hungry, New-Yorker who was ready to get in bed professionally with all kinds of people in order to be part (on the architecture side) of somewhat shady real estate deals. Cobb met the challenge head on by doing the most American thing possible: he set out to turn the school around during his five-year tenure, the exact amount of time he allowed himself to stay away from his practice.[5]

Admitting that a school can indeed be turned around in the space of five years, (an assumption bought primarily by Americans that non-American find somewhat absurd), many confirm that by the time he left in five years' time, the mood had changed and people felt more positive about themselves and the school's own status. What had happened in the *interim* was rather unprecedented: a person

---

The John Hancock Tower affair, which in fact dragged on for most the 1970s, cast a dark shadow over the city, its architect and the Pei firm at large. It needed to be washed away. As mentioned, the school had been in a state of disrepair following Sert's departure and an opportunity was up for grabs to do what is expected by members, like Cobb, of the American aristocracy: give back, which normally means doing something that may be perceived (and sold as a marketing tool for the benefit of the social status of the giver) as working for the greater good by usually implementing a somewhat paternalistic approach.

5. This was definitely a first as every other chairperson, before or after, has always stayed on in a tenured capacity.

who had been foreign to power and policy games that characterize the academic environment around the world for his whole life, he had managed to create a sense of excitement as a result of his activities—investing the school with a sense of 'intellectual discomfort' that bordered on the personal.

Of course, discomfort could not really be embraced as a significant goal in itself in an educational institutional program and Cobb was indeed not setting out to make people miserable just for the sake of doing so. The importance of discomfort was due to the fact that it reflected a personal condition of disequilibrium. It had to do with his own experience as a student, the one described in the epigraph. However, it also involved the disequilibrium which typically characterizes the life of an architect that is not exactly 'advertised' (or made evident) to people considering life in a profession that is closer to a mission than a 'profession.' The one thing that Cobb entered the school with was an awareness of such anxiety, as well as the extremely high levels of anxiety (that are usually underplayed if not hidden under the rug altogether) that tend to exist in architecture programs, especially architecture programs like Harvard's which take the form of a graduate program within a university. In his mind, several factors contribute to the anxiety found among both students and faculty at the GSD, quite independent of anything under the chairman's control. His thesis still makes a lot of sense and it is worth recalling. It goes as follows.

A condition of anxiety is produced among students because, as graduate students, they have reached quite a mature level of development in other fields before deciding to enter architectural studies. These people, therefore, have to enter a field in which the training methodology is necessarily very different from the methodology that characterizes education in academic fields. They naturally experience a certain kind of frustration, combined with anxiety, once they discover that the often highly developed interlinks and bodies of knowledge that they bring with them to the school are not terribly useful in this activity and may be counterproductive in reality. They feel a sense of loss and deprivation, in a way, as everything they have done previously turns out to be useless.

On the other hand, they find themselves plunged into an activity in which they lack the elementary skills, so that they basically have to go back to kindergarten, metaphorically speaking. This is very hard for people who are relatively mature and might like to feel that they have progressed beyond all that. The equally acute anxiety level of faculty stems from a different but related circumstance, a sort of unresolved Catch-22 to teaching in an architecture program, particularly at Harvard: universities like Harvard have become great by the way they combine a commitment to what is called general education for undergraduates with a commitment to specialized training for graduate students, as well as being dedicated to advanced research by faculty. It is the chemistry between those three activities that makes a great university.

Unfortunately, as Cobb was quick to point out, that particular chemistry does not operate in a school of architecture. This is because, in a certain way, two out of three of those elements are missing. On top of a lack of commitment to make architecture accessible to undergraduates, there is the much more serious and irresolvable problem: at the other end of that tripartite activity, the university—and this is a condition unique to architecture—cannot be the locus of advanced research, except in a very limited sense. Contrary to what people involved in academia believe, research in architecture can only take place in practice. Hence the Catch-22 that the faculty face: they cannot have what the university has to offer. All they get is the teaching load. Because it is studio based, it is so demanding and it deprives them of any significant time to do anything else, either academic research or architectural practice. On the one hand, they cannot advance in the faculty hierarchy at Harvard unless they are teaching, and their teaching needs to be well-regarded. On the other hand, if they are teaching and their teaching is well-regarded, it is usually because their intense commitment does not allow them to do anything else, or little else, and certainly not enough to acquire the stature that Harvard demands in order for a faculty member to be considered for tenure.

As is well-known, this Catch-22 dilemma is not talked about often and therefore it is not always immediately apparent to new graduates who usually imagine that their career development is assured by having an appointment at Harvard. In contrast, precisely by doing what they do so well, they are actually depriving themselves of the kind of activity that would enable them to acquire tenure. In other fields, a positive aspect of tenure is that it makes a professor a member of a well-respected community of scholars. Yet, this is not in place at the design school because the school is not involved in general education and it is not a base for significant research in the field.

As if this was not enough, a further problem increases anxiety. While it is quite difficult to get tenure, there is the added problem that being a tenured professor at the GSD does not carry with it the kind of access to one's intellectual peers that it does in other fields. As a result, Cobb states that the school is 'isolated from the life of the university, and the need to overcome that condition and the importance and benefits to both architecture and the university of overcoming it, is not exactly a popular topic of conversation. This accounts for the great deal of discomfort already in place in the psyches of both students and faculty.'

Being faced with that, if someone deliberately creates a condition that keeps increasing anxiety and discomfort, should this person then be considered irresponsible? Before answering, the following words from Cobb himself should be considered. 'The siren song of academia, combined with the anxiety stemming from the Catch-22 situation, lures faculty into a kind of understandable but in the end misbegotten effort to somehow "mimic" the university. Architecture is a field with a very weak knowledge base and it is surrounded in a university by fields with very strong knowledge bases, so it's understandable that an architecture faculty would try to pretend, in a way, to a knowledge base.'

In order to deal with this unresolvable and unusual dilemma, it meant that Cobb set out one single agenda: strengthen the relationship between teaching and studio practice by acknowledging that, in fact, research can only take place through practice in the architectural field. To do that, namely to reconnect the school to practice, he envisioned one way: greatly enhance the number of visiting critics. 'It is obvious,' he once said, 'when you think about the history of architectural education, that architecture has always had this problem in relation to the academic world because it is not the site of advanced research, but only the site of training for academic work. One cannot combine in a school of architecture what one automatically get in a school of medicine, for example, where one gets the most rigorous training in the knowledge base of the field and at the same time one get the exposure, by way of teaching hospitals, to the most advanced and original thinking in the field. It's obvious that architecture doesn't work that way and it is a huge dilemma.'

It is important to remember that, at the time, seventy percent of the faculty at most state university schools of architecture were tenured, and they were mostly resistant to all sorts of 'change,' especially policy change. Yet, Cobb did not have to face this problem thanks to the twofold clearing of the way done by his predecessor (Mc Cue), both as a chairman (by starting to clear away the dead wood from the permanent faculty, which was understaffed when Cobb entered the school), and then as dean, by creating a system of governance in which the tenured faculty did not have the kind of control present in most academic departments.[6]

---

6. People unfamiliar with American academia might be unaware that a specific, well thought-out structure of power and responsibility had been historically designed to ensure that the University works as a cloak. Each school is run by a dean who traditionally (read: up until the XXI century) is responsible for the administration, fund raising and nomination of the chair-person of each departments. The department chair, in turn, is traditionally responsible for the intellectual project, which meant inviting visiting critics to the GSD, the guest lecturers select the shows and set the cultural goals of the Harvard Design Magazine. This clear, well-oiled structure began to be radically altered after 2007 by the second-to-last dean. As a member of a minority group, he decided it was time to be in charge of everything—lecture program, magazine, visitors and faculty appointment—leaving most faculty members uncertain about the role and the need of having chair persons in the first place, but certain about the importance of not challenging the 'dean revolution' in any overt fashion. That particular dean was allowed to carry out this unprecedented change because he had managed, during his appointment negotiation, to convince the first-ever female University President (nominated as a result of the politically incorrect statements regarding female scientists voiced by her predecessor, the former Treasury Secretary of the Clinton administration) that

In other words, Cobb was given *carte blanche,* which meant he could silently embrace pluralism by bringing it in behind the often freezing policy discussion that characterizes most academic activity. A diverse and sometimes bizarre world (that is sometimes described as an underworld) started to surface not just for the sake of diversity, but to expose the student body to that mood of destabilization and anxiety that so heavily characterizes the world of a practicing architect.[7]

The 1980s were the height of the modern-postmodern debate, a debate which was largely absent from the school. Cobb's response was to promote the debate by inviting people who were on one side of that debate to teach in the core program. This would allow students to get the benefit of being later exposed to other voices from the contrasting side through the optional program. He also began to lay the groundwork for reinstituting the thesis. This move encountered fierce opposition from both students and faculty.

These actions did create discomfort, yet it was not the end. Instead, it was a necessary consequence of the effort to create a certain mood. 'It was more a mood than anything else,' Cobb said, 'but, of course, the substance was important. The glory days of Harvard were perceived to have been those when so-called foreigners were running

---

this was a good idea. The proposal also included expanding the size of his physical office. In other words, Harvard, like all American institutions, has recently decided that the tyrannies of minorities, political correctness and digital leadership trump everything else, competence and precedent included.

7. The reader interested in the atmosphere of the school during Cobb's tenure can refer to the piece titled A silent symposium, Meetings with Harvard professors published in the present anthology.

the school. Its international reputation was based on the perception that Harvard was reaching out to and engaging a larger world.'

Concurrently his appointment was also very purposefully aimed at reconnecting the school to the American profession. 'The single most purposeful program of visitors that I had was to bring Chicago architects to the GSD because I felt that Harvard had always turned its back on Chicago, and vice versa, and that somehow Chicago is the one city in North America that, more than any other place, is the place to be engaged. What I wanted to show was that Chicago was the city in which the culture of architecture was sufficiently well established that a kind of debate could take place there through practice, and Chicago embraced that idea that architecture is actually making a contribution to the culture through the way it is practiced. The way to demonstrate that, in my view, was to bring Chicago architects who knew each other, who were building and who brought very different points of view to the school. I think it worked pretty well and it did overcome to a large degree the sense of isolation, or alienation, between Harvard and the Midwest.'

The combination appeared 'destabilizing' to some, but not to Cobb. Perhaps because of his background and the sense of familiarity he had with the institution, he strongly believed that one of the obligations that falls on powerful institutions—and none is more powerful than Harvard—is to expose itself to destabilization, precisely because they are powerful. They can tolerate it and not be destroyed.

'Harvard is Harvard. People want to come from all over the place. How could I have gotten all those people from another institution? People want to come because they want to get their portion of stage there. I think it is correct to characterize my role at the GSD as being an *impresario*! That is what I was. Because I am the preeminent example of an instrumental architect or, if you will, a member of an instrumental practice. I respond to projects that are brought to me and, for me, that is what architecture is! Now, does it mean that it is not possible to elevate it beyond the merely instrumental? No, it does not but my mode of operation is instrumental and not theoretical. It is completely instrumental, even though I would like to think that sometimes throughout the instrumental mode I could raise it to a level that has theoretical interest.'

Post scriptum

Many people familiar with academic environments around the world confirm privately that it is exactly this impresario attitude which is needed the most in academia at the present juncture, even though they remain sceptical about whether it has a real shot at succeeding in being implemented today.

Meetings with Harvard Professors. A Silent Symposium

New York City, 1999. Unpublished

The following piece gathers notes taken during a series of interviews conducted with people equipped with first-hand knowledge of Cobb's chairmanship for the simple reason that they were active participants in it. It arguably appears as too biased today, with no room left for more incendiary recollections like the one that Mr Eisenmann may have uttered, for instance. However, it is included and it seemingly manages to convey both a sense of the mood at the school in the 1980s and offer a behind-the-curtain look at some of the hidden facets of the academic world that are rarely discussed.

1.

I enter the HGSD—Harvard Graduate School of Design—at noontime, on a rather cold February Wednesday. My first appointment is scheduled for 2:00 p.m. There is some time to check minor details related to my upcoming activity: that is, to meet with Harvard professors of architecture or, for that matter, urban planning, who had been involved in one way or another with Cobb's HGSD Chairmanship, and exchange opinions on it. I am determined to ask them all the very same set of questions, even though they do not know it: I am after what one could call *a silent symposium* where each participant can deliver his own recollection of the period under investigation without being influenced by the replies of others. Public symposiums require a lot of time to be organized, which I do not have. Nor do the speakers. Public symposiums, furthermore, are more and more less interesting than they used to be. Participants either repeat second-hand opinions, or blame each other, often in a sensational way.

Even though the topic at hand, Cobb as chairman and teacher, is unlikely to provoke anything of the kind, this is a different symposium altogether. Since we would need to talk about things past, no attempt to produce coherent recollection will be made. It is a long time since Anna Achmatova taught us that "every attempt to produce coherent memories amounts to falsification. No human memory is so arranged as to recollect everything in continues sequence. Letters and diaries often turn out to be bad assistants."

This silent symposium, then, excludes at the outset pre-orchestrated opinions. No document will be at hand, no previous attention has been directed to specific issues. A *festansprache* more than a *festschrift*. The truth of the matter is that, to approach Cobb the architect, one needs to consider his "academic foot." One would need to measure it, comparing it with his other foot, the one of the practitioner, as each one, if deprived of the other, would put under a deceptive light his entire career. The latter would appear affected by a limp, while this is hardly the case.

The consequence: four individuals are involved. Some of them even ignore the topic of the discussion. They form a cross-section of the school—a group of people with first-hand knowledge of the experience under investigation who have demonstrated a huge commitment to the University and for whom the letter H has come to house a particular place in the personal alphabet of their own lives. In fact, each of them spent more time at the HGSD than Cobb himself: this is what links together individuals otherwise equipped with distinct age, career, goals, and personas.

2.

The first one on the agenda is Preston Scott Cohen, a student during Cobb's chairmanship and now a member of the so-called young faculty group—the one mainly involved with the core program. I meet with him in front of his office. In his typical way, Scott is walking back and forth, talking to somebody else.

If this is a previous appointment or just a casual member of his peripatetic confraternity, I am just not able to tell. After a while, we shake hands. When we enter his room, the state of disarray is such that no seats are in sight. His work station appears to be very much *in sintonia* with student work stations. We decide to look for another place: the most probable candidate appears to be the windowless, and therefore, dark, silent, and, for a change, unoccupied

Piper Auditorium. We go there. During this room-search time, I inform Scott about the purpose of my visit. Simply put: to gather opinions and information about Cobb as a teacher of architecture and, above all, to discuss his impact upon the school as a chairman. Scott looks interested. Scott came to HGSD in 1983: "I came in when he decided to do something that would shake the school. I came in the door right at the moment he decided to do that."

Scott was a member of the second Eisenman studio series—a hot potato by any standard—and participant in many other hot, hot discussions under way at the time. About the individual who made those happenings possible, Scott is unambiguous: "It was Harry's beautiful idea, to bring in these extremely radical persons... there will be a connection with Rossi that Eisenman would have been written about... the whole IAUS culture was something that Harry must have been captivated by.

And those people were at the end of their academic efforts and becoming important players in the profession. Harry started that tradition of lunch-interviews, by asking Eisenman to do that."

But this is just a flourishing of thought and images. Then we return to the influence that Cobb had on the school. Although he does not have any first-hand knowledge of the HGSD in the 1970s, Scott firmly believes that it is possible to talk of a pre-Cobb and a post-Cobb era at the HGSD, the one the school is still in. "I do feel that we are still in a period which begins with Harry. And it always seems to me that there is a pre-Harry period and a post-Harry period. I feel like he is *the* modern chairman of this school. I do not know if this is true, but this is my impression."

From the way he talks about it, I decode it as a state of mind: an atmosphere of confrontation and dialogue. But also a place where the intellect is a constant object of *stimulii*: and, maybe, too many of them. The account of some of the more acute peaks of reviews goes far beyond anything which anyone had ever described to me in spoken words; the recollection of them is still vivid and present in Scott's memory. "He built the idea of skepticism as being the key to intellectual activity. Harry built the idea of having a leader who, instead of leading the way, brought a particular combination of contesting parties. That made Harvard important again. Many people were unhappy about it, they thought there was too much instability. The amazing thing about Harry is that he could talk to everyone, no matter what they were talking about. He could enter a discussion and make a contribution we all cared about, which is amazing, because, usually, you do respect one party or the other, but no matter which side Harry spoke to, each side would still listen. That is unusual. He is an unusual man. Everyone revered him."

At this point I feel compelled to ask him to draw a brief profile of ..."Of Henry Cobb?" Scott interrupts me. He laughs hysterically and then says "I wish I could hear what the others answer. What would Jorge [Silvetti] say?" After that he ponders about Cobb's voice. "I should say something about his voice. Somebody that you can always be sure of will say things with care but at the same time they will be very compelling to listen to. He is not someone who relies on saying things that you only want to hear and that would be careful and reassuring because of its wisdom, which also comes with something you are just waiting to listen to, you know, you have to wait for them because of the slowness with which he speaks, which I think is very important, by the way; this anticipation of the things he would say and the fact that they are always a remarkable combination in a way of long views of a wisdom man, forward looking, ongoing thinking..." I prevent the entering of any flattering area by telling him about the comment that Moneo made when he was appointed.

My question: "Moneo said that he was very happy to become chairman because he knew what Harvard meant throughout the world. Do you know what that is?" Scott's reply: "Well I think it is an observation about the status of the school. The question of the status of the school is mainly associated with the question of respect, authority, or inventiveness. One of Harry's most beautiful comments was at his opening lecture as a chairman, a lecture about balancing audacity, openness, coherence, rigor. I think that would be the way he would like to think of Harvard doing that, and being respected because of all that. I think that is what Moneo meant and what Harry would subscribe. But also the privileges that are associated with its status. No one can deny that. And the privilege means that we have licenses that other schools may not have. But also there is a solidity, a reliability, it is question about foundations, about permanence, immutability; there is something about Harvard that tends to represent that status. Even if he brought in other critical voices, he would never bring them in to the point that they would dominate, I would imagine."

At this point, I am tempted to ask whether this time is a real historical past to him, but Scott precedes me. Talking about the relationship between theory and practice, asking himself whether or not there a possibility for theory to be instrumental, Scott judges Cobb's skepticism as "having to do with what I call his critical eyes." Scott's point: "Now we have seen that theory operates within different aspects of our field; it is not an autonomous piece, but there might be theoretical questions inherent in historical investigations, already inside of history, and this point of view should not be contemned. Inside the question of representation, there will always be a theoretical problem. Inside of technology in that very field there need to be inquiries which might be called theoretical as well. I think that the relationship between history and theory would be better worked out, by talking about an organic relationship between theory, practice and history. And I am not sure which one would I put before the other. One needs to draw to get immersed in the technical, one needs a theoretical hypothesis, and one needs the history to provide the basis to undertake the work. That kind of work, place this question in a very different way.

I would hope it would be resolved without polar oppositions between practice and theory. I think that we should be over the question of dual oppositions like that. I think it is not any more that way. Maybe in Harry's time it needed to be put that way. Very didactic. But I think the relationship has evolved since then. It is starting from his time that theory evolved, when a theory course became a required course, I think. Giorgio Ciucci was invited here to give a course on treatises. So it is history and practice, theory did not have its own life so much. It was the theory of architecture and the history of architecture, it was not theory with its own history. Architects brought theory to architecture.

That was why he brought Peter Eisenman here, or Libenskind. The question is whether Libenskind is an architect or not. What Harry did was to bring people who practice architecture in a manner that, theoretically speaking, might be questioning the very nature of the discipline, by means of theoretical inquiries. Now you have to draw from outside of profession to stimulate thought!"

"The out-of-towners?" I ask promptly.

"Yes, the out-of-towners. Tourists. People who might not be the most effective movers of ideas in their fields become so in architecture. Architecture welcomes them because of anxieties, and some lack of confidence about its ambition. But, again, I think that Harry's time was different. There was more confidence; he built a school which had a confidence about its mission so that it was able to accept architects who brought theoretical questions. I think that it is unfortunate that there is not more than that: there is less stimulation coming from within. People who made that case wanted to move to become powerful practitioners of the Harry Cobb variety; even he is not willing to recognize what he did with the Hancock building..."

This topic brings us to the professional dimension of architecture. Asked about this, and about the fact of having a school of architecture within an university setting, Scott thinks that "a school of architecture should be within a university setting, but there is still the dilemma of what are we able to produce. The question of the autonomy of the discipline: whether or not in its particularity architecture is becoming a bridge, or a catalyst making connection with other bodies of knowledge, is sort of unclear. It is a sort of undecided situation we are left in.

Architecture neither proclaims itself as a specific area of knowledge with which the university needs to contend with, nor has it been able to have a central enough position to bring things into a perception that make them of interest. I am not sure this has been resolved at all. The school is still segregated from the world of practice. I dare say the topic has ever hardly been discussed. No one cares. It is also a problem of technology. Because of the advance of technology, the manner in which the school has been able to absorb that into design is very problematic. The school has a great difficulty with technology, actually. No matter how much attention has been paid to it in various way in its department, in design is not doing well. So this disassociation with practice has increased. This is post-Harry. It is another problem, although I am sure it has always been that way, not being able to follow new developments. There is in fact a tendency to resist technology in design, to continue to draw by hand, for example. I have doubts about it. I would prefer that we would understand technology more."

My dialogue with Scott is abruptly stopped as we are entering an interesting topic. Scott is talking about the Hancock Tower, which "seems to be the very last significant building in this city. It is an extraordinarly modern building which has made such an important impression on such a wide audience and which contributes something that still seems so contemporary and powerful to me."

I am running out of time and I am supposed to meet the second member of this silent symposium: Jorge Silvetti, current chair of the architectue department. After having told Scott about my predicament, we exit Piper Auditorium. While doing so, we come across Mack Scogin, former chair of the same department, who is taking a break from some review, so I gather. As he is fairly interested by our unexpected appearance, and arguably in the mood for some chatting, the three of us start an informal talk. Scott informs Scogin about our activity. Scogin expresses right away his absolute admiration for the Hancock Tower. As a curious coincidence, Scogin is teaching a course based on a thorough investigation of the Copley Square area: inevitably, he looks and looks at the Hancock. The more he looks at the Hancock, the more he is struck by it. Scogin expresses some interesting thoughts about it. As much as I would like to extend this talk, I am now very late and obliged to leave. We shake hands. I jump on a cab and instruct the driver about my destination. On our way to Jorge's office, we hit Copley Square. It is now late in the afternoon and the sun has come out powerfully. Having been inside since noon, I now realize what a beautiful day this has become. The Hancock is now nothing less than a *raggio di sole* amplifying the intense luminosity of the dying sun. "The vertical cousin to the horizontal huge blueness of the sea" as Updike described it in a short story, is now a refraction of light, advertising the natural event all over the Boston area. Another way of melting into the sky. "Is it not magnificent?" are the words erupting, all of the sudden from the driver's mouth. "You are totally right" is all I am able to say, nodding my head.

Shortly after, we stop at Silvetti's office. I enter and ask for a glass of water while waiting for Silvetti, who is reviewing some design developments. When we meet I am informed about his tight window: he has a meeting to attend in less than an hour. We start right away. I inform him about Scott's thesis of the pre-Cobb and post-Cobb eras. He agrees, while articulating it further. Having come to the school in 1975 as an assistant professor, Silvetti witnessed the transformation of the school. On his career: "I was promoted to associate professor in 1978. I was teaching in the core studio, studio options and the first required course of theory in this country." About the school in the 1970s, Silvetti has few hesitations. Silvetti describes the school in the 1970s "as being in a state of disarray. When I got here in 1975, the situation was so bad that, after a semester, I was about to resign. I saw it as a backward place. I was very unhappy. It acutely exploded when I came here. It was very, very bad until McCue came. It was very uninspiring and very unproductive.

There was no theory at all. No acceptance of basic ideas that were being discussed at the time like, say, Venturi or the New York Five. Nobody knew who Tafuri was!"

Silvetti agrees with me in saying that, by 1985, the school was again one of the more important in the country. In fairness, though, Silvetti would not attribute that to Cobb alone. Silvetti talks of a *duetto*: Cobb-McCue. He says that McCue is the one who did the house-cleaning and, in a way, paved the way to the 1980s transformation "establishing a policy of appointments and promotions that did not exist before, and, above all, establishing an atmosphere of fairness, creating real opportunities for younger people. My case is emblematic, in that respect." "Before that," Silvetti goes on, "the school was ruled in an authoritarian way by senior faculty. McCue truly democratized the structure of the school, allowing for the arrival of new ideas and people. What Harry did was to operate within that structure and use it in the most intelligent way. That is to say, to bring the school to the fore, by bringing all the people and the diversity of ideas he brought, transforming the school into a forum of ideas at an international level, something that school has always been, and that was dismissed in the seventies." Asked about the Cobb's understanding of Harvard, Silvetti defines it as an attempt "to keep the international profile of the school. That is the strength! And I think we are trying to maintain that. It is also what happened with Gropius and Sert times. Certain schools tend to be associated with a certain types of geography. There are schools that are very American, there are schools that are very English, because of associations, past relationships. Harvard is indisputably a school that has always been international. Today a lot of schools are very international too, but that is the Harvard lesson, in a way."

About the atmosphere in the early 1980s, Silvetti agrees with Scott: "In order to broaden the discussion, and given his interest in dialogue, Harry brought to the school very disparate personalities. In a way he set the tone in which we are still today. An undogmatic and very productive one, very healthy. It represented the state of architecture. It was not definable as a school of thought but rather defined by a discourse about architecture that was approached from many directions. In that sense it was as it was in the fifties, at the forefront: because it represented the state of architecture with its more advanced ideas. I think Harry well articulated that at an intellectual level but also intuitively because, you should know, it was not very clear at the time. As usual, you understand what is happening only in retrospect. He took risks."

As if to confirm this by way of an example, Silvetti says that he was concerned about Cobb's appointment. "In the late seventies, a chairman search was set. I was not part of it because I was a junior faculty. But when McCue announced his choice, we—the junior faculty—expressed our concerns and even our non-support for a person like Harry. Living in New York, and coming on a part-time basis, he did not appear to us as the right person to perform such a demanding task. I was prepared for a disaster. To my delight, I can now say that I was completely wrong! Even though Harry did definitely keep one of his feet in New York, whatever time he spent here, considering the intensity with which he put this place in motion, he seemed as if he were here full time. It was really amazing. Really amazing. I am so happy that I was so wrong! And I have told him."

Stimulated by my desire to know more about the changes in the curriculum, Jorge says: "Harry did two things that changed the curriculum very much . He added a fourth semester to the core and made the thesis project mandatory."

To this, I replied my own dissatisfaction with thesis projects in general, as they seem to be less conclusive and focused than studio projects. His position: "The thesis is independent work. It has to be judged on its own terms. It is the first important statement by a young architect. It is not a tutorial. The advisor is just a critic. In that sense it is incredibly successful. Of course we are tough, but this is our role." The core transformation represents to Silvetti a more painful topic because of certain appointments done by Cobb. In particular, Silvetti had "tremendous problems with Bahram Shirdel." Jorge talks about him as a misfit. If the shoe does not fit, Jorge believes, it is no use saying that time and wear will make it more comfortable, or that the shape could be altered, or that the pain is an illusion. "Shirdel would not accept the terms of the core program," Silvetti says. "On the day the program (tailored on the notion of the site) was presented to students, Shirdel announced that he did not have a site, because he does not believe in it, or, above all, in a course that is about site. That created some tension. I do not think that his presence was stimulating. It was more a problem than anything else."

On the Peter Eisenman *affaire* Silvetti is lapidarian: "I suggested to him to bring Peter Eisenman. I have always been very interested in his manipulation of forms."

After that we have an extended conversation on the 1985 Walter Gropius Lecture and the "misfit dilemma." The level of excitement in Silvetti is now evidently high. From his tone, I gather that the issue is still of crucial importance to him. His words: "Architecture *must* and *can* only operate within a university setting, because it a unique mode of producing knowledge that is not only valuable but necessary. It is one of the few disciplines that can handle completely incompatible and heterogeneous masses of information. I do not think that there are other discipline that can do that. We are not dealing with scientific or scholarly method, but with a way of thinking and looking at the world, being able to seize the sight of it in different modes. That was the political agenda in his Gropius Lecture. He was telling the university that we are important and that they had better consider us as such. I do believe more and more in graduate education. We are still *an* education. We educate people in a broad way. And there is nothing better than a university setting to do that. Simply because you cannot offer everything. A great thing that Harry did was to establish full time appointments of history of architecture. All of us believe that the grounding of knowledge in history is absolutely indispensable. From the purely scholarly and architectural point of view, there is nothing worse than having an architect that ignore the history of the discipline. It is actually dangerous!"

Inevitably, this leads him to speculate on Gropius a bit further. After having taken a long breath: "If you think about it," Silvetti ponders, "this is very interesting, reflecting on his own education. The awareness of that, the lack of history in his own days is very interesting. A lot of people, particularly famous architects, are inclined to repeat what they were taught. When faced with the problem of teaching, they become very conservative. They say 'Well, I was taught this way, and of course, I am so good that I do not see the need to change all this.' Harry, on the contrary, had no prejudice in actually going against all of these things, even though he came from the strongest school of the time.

This was amazingly refreshing. It actually broke down all our prejudices. We were very suspicious of his Gropius education—something he was very critical about. Much more than us. In fact, contrary to expectations, he started to do all he did because he was very critical about it. He never mystified his education. He never used it as an example; instead, he used to laugh about it."

No more time being available, this is the last thing said. I accompany Jorge to his appointment in a taxi cab. Interestingly enough, the Hancock shows its head again. We both agree on the fact that there is room for a book on it, a good one where, to Scott's dismay, out-of-towners (not architecturally trained critics) play no part. Stimulated on current writing on architecture, Silvetti expresses his dismay: "I think there is a lot of charlatanism. They understand architecture as a media phenomena. They do not know the subject they are talking about. They understand it only metaphorically. Most of the time the discourse is so oblique that it is completely detached. The object is deferred." We halt on that note, adding to Scott's my own wish to hear his HNC own profile.

3.

It is now Thursday and I go back to the HGSD to make my silent symposium more fleshy. The next speaker is Eduard Sekler, whom I meet in his office. His office strikes me as the opposite of Scott's. A sense of order prevails, every book at its place, much visual material arranged for some probable upcoming lessons. Sekler came to Harvard in 1955 to teach architectural history and theory—an activity that he has performed since.

His first recollection of Cobb is when they both were on the 1969 famous first committee of Governance, when

University Hall was occupied by students. Cobb was representing alumni, Sekler was representing faculty. "We spent endless hours debating. At that time we became better known. We were trying to do something. For the best, you know. What struck me at that time was Harry's loyalty to Harvard and to the GSD in particular. Otherwise, he would not have found the time. He was not an officer. He did not have to do that. I liked him right away. Very thoughtful."

Not unexpectedly, his recollection of the 1970s is the most articulate. "The 1970s were a time when McKillbridge was the dean. He was not a designer. He was a man who came from the business school. That makes a big difference already. Sert infused a certain spirit in the school. He was a leader because of his enthusiasm. Of course he was LeCorbusier- inspired but, as you know, definitely made a contribution on his own. He was a Catalan. He brought this all Mediterranean thing that Le Corbusier admired but did not have. Sert loved cities. He brought to the school a great love for cities. After all, he invented the urban design program in this country.

One may say that, by modern standards, he probably was a very bad administrator because he did not care. So the University administration put in a good housekeeper the minute he was gone. But that was not good for the design faculty. That was one factor. Then we had George Anselevichius as a chairman. He just did not have the stature for that kind of leadership. Fortunately we still had very good faculty, people of substance. The turnaround was when McCue became chairman. Here we had again somebody of substance. McCue came with a good record from Berkeley and became a powerful leading figure. He understood what it means to build up not only a department but a school. He become dean, as you know, and really built up the school.

To give you an example, when McCue came, there was one endowed chair. When he stepped out, we had ten endowed chairs. He had, of course, the intuition and the power of persuasion of getting HArry Cobb, a respected designer equipped with authority who cared about Harvard, to serve as chairman. Harry had a real feeling for the University. It meant something to him. He also understood New England tradition very well. He belongs there. What is very clear now is that he opened the school up to what was going on at the time. Whether or not one approved of it, one had to know about it, and above all one had to come to terms with it. And so we had a time of very interesting discussions; in committee, among faculty, or individually.

On the by now well advertised "misfit" Sekler is clarifying: "There was an administrative struggle at the time between us, faculty, and Bok [Harvard University president] about the place of a professional school. The University did not prohibit professors in medical school practicing medicine. In fact, you have over there fifty medical professors. For the practice of architecture, there is no room left for the administration of the university. You are supposed to do that on the side. It is a question of time allotment. If you are a full-time professor you do not have the time to do anything else. Bok would say that lawyers are not allowed to practice while teaching. If they want to practice, they would need to go part-time. There is the misfit. We were trying to convince the administration: you do not forbid a scientist to have his laboratory within the university, but for the architect the laboratory is the building. That has not been resolved, really. One of the things that came out of that was the appointment of adjunct professors. There are quite a few now. An adjunct professor is a professor in the practice of something. In fact, he is expected to practice.

And therefore, in the allotment of time, the arrangements are different. That was the real outcome. Generally speaking, the notion of having a school of design within a university setting, goes back to the nineteenth century, to Norton: the fact that architecture was part of education. Unfortunately, that has been lost, at present, again. It has been removed from the syllabus of the Carpenter Center. It has been eradicated. It will come back again. It goes in waves."

When asked about the function of architectural theory and criticism, and informed about Cobb's skepticism, Sekler can only reply by handing me a copy of *Connection*, a Harvard publication from 1968. There one can read that "Architectural theory, as a contemplative pursuit, becomes a personal search for basic assumptions about architecture and, of necessity, about more than architecture since it must engage the total human being in order to arrive at authentic results." It is what Sekler still believes.

To interview the last member of this silent symposium, Alex Krieger, is, from Sekler's office, a matter of one floor up. Krieger, now Urban Design Program Coordinator, was an HGSD urban design student between 1975 and 1977, became a visiting critic after that, and got hired as an assistant professor in 1980. He consequently become Cobb's associate chair. Even though he was a student in the 1970s, Krieger does not have a clear recollection of it. His point: "When you're a student at the GSD it's hard for you to confess that it's the low point in the history of the school. I didn't feel that way when I was a student here. Nonetheless, I now think it is true and the reasons are rather complex. It's a little bit of what MIT has been going through in recent years. The reign of Sert and his immediate successors had come to an end, there was a bit of a vacuum and so it was the end of a very strong era, so there was a bit of a lull, and that led to the perception that it was on the down side of its rise. And there was an unfortunate appointment of a dean that did not work out very well. [...] Gerry [Mc Cue] and Harry were very important, but there was a natural shift and gap in epochs, and certainly Gerry and Harry were the next epoch, and before them there was a lull, that's for sure. I don't think to the world at large this big lull was as apparent as it was internally. I don't believe people had written off the GSD in 1976 as no longer being an important school."

By this Krieger means that HNC and McCue were a very interesting pair. To explain this: "While Harry was always quite supportive of the additional structure and rigor that was Gerry McCue's natural proclivity, I think he understood the limitations of it. And so he would occasionally throw that stone to create a ripple. So he was at the same time creating a structure and throwing stones. There was great skepticism about Harry's arrival. Very few of the academicians felt it was a good choice, because they assumed that Harry was coming from the world of practice and would shift the discussion away from theory and history and reflective aspects of the field towards a more professional orientation. The fear was heightened because that was always the fear about Gerald McCue, so here's Gerald McCue hiring a distinguished practitioner, but not a distinguished academician, so that fear was compounded by the choice. Maybe in part Harry was sensitive to that skepticism, and perhaps some of the choices he made about bringing others in were to challenge that. Harry acted against what some people's expectations were. He opened the door to theory, which, prior to Harry, was a not entirely legitimate activity. It was always considered somehow subordinate to history, and Harry opened the door to theory as being the equal of history. And in that sense the array of history/theory courses increased, but I would not say that there was not a history component before. History had been coming back slowly since the nadir much earlier, probably when Harry was a student here." I interrupt him by saying: "In the 40s it was banished...." "That's right," Krieger continues, "and he likes to reflect upon that, but it had steadily come back and was very much in place, but in a more orthodox sense of you start by studying antiquities and you work your way through the historical periods. It was more like art history, the history of art and architecture. The notion of history and the notion that you could study *modern* architecture and in that case the schism between history and theory had to be addressed. So Harry's contribution was legitimizing the role of history/theory."

This formulation leads Krieger to an interesting, personal understanding: "I think Harry used his years here in a wonderful personal way, independent of the effect on the school, of getting his own ghosts out. That if you are sceptical of theory or contemporary discussion about architecture, he was going to challenge his own scepticism through the activities of the school. If he was a lifelong practitioner fully committed to that enterprise during these years, he was going to come to a greater personal understanding about the value of a pedagogy versus training or practice. So I think that independent of the effect on the school, he used it in a wonderful way of challenging his own limitations and reservations and beliefs about the field. So part of what we benefit from is that self-reflective-ness that occurred in his own mind during those years."

My next question is then this: "Is this also due to the restoration of the thesis program?" Krieger: "I believe so.

The thesis option had waned in the preceding decades and it was an option that was not selected very frequently. I assume Harry was instrumental in restoring it. Actually, there were steps taken at two ends of the curriculum, and the sum total of the two steps was more significant than either one. At one end there was a statement saying that a thesis would become mandatory and that it be a serious piece of independent work that in a sense prepared the student for the transition from school to practice. At the same time, the core program was strengthened. It was re-evaluated, the principles behind the core were reconsidered, the relationship between the support courses, they're sometimes called—technology and structures and so forth—and design was re-conceptualized and another core studio was added. So what happened in a matter of a couple of years was that a program that had been three core studios and four optional studios shifted to becoming four core studios and a thesis, making the option program down to two instead of four. That made a substantial change in the rigor of the place. It also created the need for a slightly larger in-house faculty, because before that there was a greater array of visitors. So it had percolation throughout the system. I would say both things were significant."

The flowering of positions everybody refers to—the bold, creative, numerous, influential experiments in representation underway at the school in the first part of the 1980s; their various tributaries and confluences in architectural debate—this vast amalgam seems to have nourished the school up until now. As to stimulate the nerves a bit further, I move the discussion toward what Alex describes as *a big stone to be thrown into the pool*: the Eisenman appointment. "That was an appointment that sort of destabilized the security of some people. It offended some others. Sekler thought it was inappropriate, Silvetti was threatened by him. I don't think that McCue believe it was such a good idea. I was not senior at the time. But the sense to us, was that just at the moment the school was raising itself, there was this destabilizing force that was been brought into the school. Peter Eisenman was the most famous because of his personality, but, you see, some people mistook Harry's interest in Peter Eisenman as being more profound than it was. Harry wanted to surround himself and he felt that the students should be exposed to a mix of people with very strong opinions. Eisenman was one, but then he invited Leon Krier to battle him, which he did; he invited Libenskind, Christopher Alexander, Rossi. The animosity was just terrific. But those were of course visitors, and with Eisenman there was an attempt to make a senior appointment that was eventually denied."

Before I can add something, Krieger goes on to depict the appointments policy: it is the most articulated recollection of Shirdel's activity."There was another appointment that had actually far more percolation through the school and that was Bahram Shirdel. If there was, in my opinion, a sort of a cataclysmic event that actually helped undo Harry in part as well as establish his interests, realm of ideas, it was that appointment. Shirdel was hired as an assistant professor and thrown into the midst of the third semester studio. That studio was McKinnell's studio. It was called Column and Mechanical. All right. People knew that in the third semester they would know about real things, columns and beams, not purely from an engineer point, but as a source of inspiration for architecture. And if you look at the catalogue of the time, you realize that they had a theme for the course, something that we do not have at all now. The theme was: the bones of the building, not literally, but you know what I mean. So we were all good guys dealing with the nature of the wall, the nature of the structure, serial compositions and all those things that were very important to McKinnell at the time. In the midst of this, one the most disciplined course of the school, Bahram Shirdel was thrown in, starting those amazing purely formal transformations, taking a plan, cutting a section through it, making a section plan, and all this interesting but also amazingly sort of systematic formal transformations. That was much more threatening to the school than Peter Eisenman. Much more. First of all, it affected the core. And secondly because, unlike with Peter, here was a method with which to produce complexity. All of a sudden, whether you were a good student or a bad student, in a matter of days you could produce the most amazingly complicated Libenskind-like drawing. And the more you do it, the more remarkable it is. And then, you cut it out, you put it in front of a light, and you get flashing and you get shadows on the wall and you get some fantastic light show. Meanwhile, the other students are drawing 20 by 20 foot base and estimate whether or not they should put a round column. That thing collapsed. Shirdel was very brave. He was like bees and honey with the students. You did not need to listen anymore to some sort of conventional presentation, you were immediately able to have a virtuosity in producing form. Of course, very good students and very bad students flocked to Shirdel. And so, for a couple of years it did undermine part of the discipline of the core. Probably it took to much more greater degree than Harry thought. It was like a virus spreading through the school. It took Moneo to evict the virus."

This brings us nonchalantly to the "Moneo comment." I use it to get Krieger to talk about the traditional role of Harvard; the international aura attached to the school but also a sort of international duty that the school is expected to perform. His position: "Yes. This is again where Harry's role was more complex. Of course, the GSD unlike, say, Yale, was less engaged with an international community, and its heart was very much in the American continent. Harvard was the opposite. MIT, on the other hand, had a similar international orientation, but more towards the developing world. Coming from Moneo, I think, is the kind of Europe-US access he was talking about, and also gave him pleasure. Not Harvard being so internationally involved, Africa and that sort of stuff, but Harvard as the main access of Western tradition. And through that access influenced other parts of the world as well. When I say that Harry played a very complex role I say that he was fully aware of that role, and yet, while he fully acknowledged the importance of this, he wanted to throw some other stones. One of the many reasons for the coming of so many practitioners from the American Midwest, was again this kind of stone: it is like saying: Harvard is fully aligned with western tradition, with Europe, and that is a fact of continuity. Harry wanted to say: that is great, but, wait a minute, there is Stanley Tigerman here, talking about Chicago. It is another example of his always trying, within a structure, to tinker with it."

As if to substantiate this, Krieger gives me an example. "Harry and Jaquelin Robertson, one of the great buddies of his, were kidding around about the East Coast orientation towards Europe; and what about the American tradition itself? And so, at one point, they envisioned this thing that did not take place, but I thought it was a wonderful commentary; they were going to create a joint lecture series at UVA and at the GSD called The Adams/Jefferson Debate. Now, you have to be an American to appreciate this, because Jefferson and Adams were great rivals across their entire career. They had great respect for each other, they both became presidents, they wrote 10,000 letters to one another and so forth. They loved each other, and hated each other. And Adams' family was of course associated with Massachusetts, Harvard, Boston while Jefferson was Virginia, UVA ecetera. So they were trying to raise the flag of America, to convey in modern terms this great intellectual debate among Americans, from two regions of the country. I spent a lot of time writing letters, asking for grands to make this thing happen, which it did not. It was an interesting kind of point for me, to show that they were equal. Almost. They were not afraid of a certain amount of parochialism, which Harvard periodically is. We are now, I would say. When you mention: shall we engage ourselves with Boston? The answer is: Oh no, that is not interesting. Now, of course it is not Europe. Now it is China, and Singapore or Typee; but Harry was not above all this. He said, you know, our interest should be Boston, the Midwest, Europe."

Having mentioned his name again, I am reminded and forced to ask him for his own profile. Shortly afterwards, Krieger says:"In a funny way he proved to be the opposite of what everybody thought he was. I think that he is a much more gifted intellect than he is a designer. His creativity lies not so much in his design ability, but in the way he tries to think through a problem. That was the most impressive part about him, in my opinion, while he was here. Equivalent to Moneo, when Harry was at a studio review—and he attended many of them—it was always full; people were always hanging on his words. Part of it is just the way he delivers his own comments and so forth, but it was remarkable. People immediately realized that he was going to say very interesting things, that he was going to ask very provocative questions, and the sense of struggling through an issue was very apparent. I would say that, as a teacher, that was his strength, other than stone throwing, and undermining an organization. It was the commitment that he seemed to have to the realm of architectural ideas. I was very moved by that. I'll tell you, when Harry was in a jury, virtually the entire school wanted to be there to listen to what he said, and how he engaged others, whether it was Rossi, or Eisenman, et cetera. That was the power of thought towards individuals, designers, struggles, that I think was his greatest contribution to the school as a teacher. Pursuing ideas." While he says that, the telephone rings. The conversation breaks off. It is almost seven o'clock, anyway.

4.

I shake hands with Krieger and leave the school filled with some more focused pictures of Cobb's Chairmanship—an affair for which the time to have any definitive picture about has probably not yet come, as some blurred spots are still in the way, and the complete evolution of its consequences is still underway. As an *hommage* to the man who helped organize so many symposia, this one is silent in the sense that it makes its own the habit of saying no more than it is needed.

It retains the conviviality of the Ancient Greeks with no music, no wine, but much conversation, where ideas are interchanged in a subterranean way; but this is unavoidable when its members are so closely related. It has at least one evident quality: to allow one to gather sufficient concurrent evidence on a way of understanding architectural education, while offering a hint of schools today by touching briefly upon some of their current struggles.

This is of course not sufficient to complete the picture of the experience under investigation, and many significant memento of it, have been left out. To name just a few of them, besides the changes in the curriculum and the cultural activity supported by Cobb the chairman, one should think of the revitalized, strong emphasis put on the Walter Gropius Lecture Series, the support of such disparate architectural magazines as *The Harvard Archi-tectural Review* or *Oppositions,* the *International Style in Perspective* symposium, that is arguably more useful to put Cobb's personality in perspective than the International Style.

As a confirmation of his complex personality, I cannot avoid reporting two striking images of him before leaving the reader to his/her own conclusions. The first one is by Sekler: "He left no doubt that there are basic principles that are still valid. Architecture cannot be just a field of wild theorizing. It is not literary criticism, it is the factuality of the building, He always stressed that, which I, of course, welcome because it is always my conviction."

The second one by Krieger: "Harry did tremendously well as a chairman. He made some mistakes that I am sure he would acknowledge, but it was an amazing period of time in the school's history, in my opinion, because of the sheer love of discussion about architecture. He once made a comment that he now denies having made. He said that 'architecture is not about things. It is about words.'

And when I asked him about it in a public gathering, he said: 'I never said that!' because he thought I was criticizing, but I was not. I remembered that as a very profound statement, because I did not mean it to say that it was about papers versus buildings, but it was about ideas as opposed to things. That was the sheer love of discussion about architecture. To me, personally, that was a marvellous statement."

Bad client/good citizen: Notes on Hancock Place

Published in San Rocco 13, 2017

Cobb candidly admitted to the author of the anthology a number of times that he 'did not have it in his fingers.' He was very much aware of this and was also at peace with the fact that he lacked the natural design skills which are customarily present in first-rate architects. Very few people find his numerous projects interesting from a design standpoint, yet there is a relevant consensus that the John Hancock tower in Boston stands out as an American masterpiece both as a design proposition and a unique, unbelievable American odyssey. This piece exhibits an agreement on the part of the author on both counts and it is intended to offer a reflection of both while offering interesting reflections on the ethical role of high-rises. It is a role that very few people are willing to acknowledge and much less discuss today.

October 1973: I.M. Pei, an architect famous for declaring that "one doesn't choose projects, one chooses clients," announces that the 10,344 (blue reflective glass) window panes wrapping the John Hancock Tower in Boston (JHT herein with) need to be replaced.

In consequence, approximately 5,000 of the original glass panes already installed have to be removed intact (later to be reused by artists). A couple of years before, on an unusually warm February day, hundreds of such window panes had been detached from the building and crashed to the sidewalk hundreds of feet below forcing police forces to close off surrounding streets. During the many long months it took to diagnose (and later repair) the tall office building (TOB herein with) engineering flaws, sheets of plywood replaced many of the missing glass windows of the building, earning it one unique nickname: *Plywood Palace*.[1]

The announcement marked the turning point of an architectural odyssey with no precedent. The JHT is to this day the tallest building in Boston and of New England. From day one, its name has been associated to hyperbole, scandals and Nation-wide debates because of the odd relationship between its father (the client) and its mother (the architect): Henry N. Cobb (HNC herein with), a born and bred Bostonian for whom the design of TOB has been a permanent preoccupation for over 60 years.

HNC usually talks about the TOB as "the preeminent monument of the XX century (American) city, an object that

1. People joked that the Hancock Tower was the world's tallest plywood building.

can be ‘a troubling and sometimes a very sorry monument.” In fact, HNC understands his career as a continuous effort to “humanize the TOB and give it the demeanor of a good citizen.” Once compared to all the other TOB he has designed on all continents, it is clear, by all standards, that the JHT represent his most important and convincing success in such battle. Despite its explicit minimalism (formalism) the JHT does not dismiss the fact that the most important factor of the TOB is the physical presence/form—and its attached place-making urban role—rather than its content. It is precisely within this dialectics that HNC has offered one of the most intense reflections on the potential of architectural form and the role of the architect in revealing the true nature of the relationship between an architect and its client. What is his reflection? For him, the JHT puts on the table an important, often overlooked, question: “Whom do buildings serve?” a question filled with moral consequences, even though his take on the ‘moral role’ of the TOB differs significantly from what is normally understood.

bad guys

Zoom back half a century. Post-war Boston (1950-60): a place in which the XX century is still absent, or kept at bay. Big players, like the Hancock company, are dormant, or focused on investing outside of Boston The city is not flourishing as a result of a bad combination of economic and social circumstances: the Irish-American controlled political machine clashing against the Yankee-driven economic community. The socio-political split prevents everyone from investing in real estate. Money is invested elsewhere. Tall buildings, or high-rises are nowhere to be seen.

In this stagnant situation, characterized by three declines—the decline of the railroad, the decline of the waterfront and the decline of the downtown—the decision to develop and build (completion in 1964) a high-rise—Prudential Center—drags, kicking and screaming, into the XX century a town, Boston, that was resisting most of its values.

Prudential tower challenges Hancock, one of the oldest and most revered Boston-based companies, to get out of its very conservatives ways and to think hard about big buildings in the Boston Area. Slapped in the face by the new tower, Hancock feels that a prompt response is needed and hires I.M. Pei (who, in turn, later turned the commission to his partner HNC) to design something to overshadow its competitor's tower, even if that means to "profane"[2] one of the most treasured Urban civic piazza in the country: Copley Square and the prominent Historic Landmark sitting in it: Trinity Church by H.H Richardson.

The location is what makes the water boil, alienating the entire Boston community against its most prominent home company. The program, too, provides little help. The program is, in fact, plain corporate America at work: to build a high-rise for the Hancock corporation that

- has to house 2 million square feet of office space
- has to be 30,000 square feet per floor
- has to be the tallest building in Boston

---

2. The office of PEI COBB FREED and Partners, as it is now called, was funded by I.M.Pei in NYC in 1948 as an architectural division of Webb and Knapp, an innovative real estate enterprise run by William Zeckendorf that created much rumor and turbulence in NY in the 1950s.

- has to bear the company name at the top
- has to be taller than the close-by Prudential Center.

The program is universally perceived as brutal, uncivilized, inappropriate. The program, in HNC's words, "expresses little beyond the absolute primacy of profit and the meanness of private interest in fulfilling their responsibilities to the public realm" and this is the reason for the architect becoming the object of collective blame and finger-pointing upon accepting to be associated with the bad guys. The architectural circle is the most offended party. Its opposition has nothing to do with the form but with the towering hulk of a building, a monstrosity out of scale with the neighborhood.[3]

In consequence, the architect becomes the target of much public critic because he is perceived as an accomplice. The architect loses overnight all the credit that his firm—the Pei's firm—has accrued in the previous 15 years with large, highly-respected projects in the country (and in Boston in particular) like the Government center master plan and, most of all, the Kennedy library, a commission that made I.M. Pei the first (pre-digital) global star of the architecture world.

---

3. I refer here to the concept of profanation in a fashion opposite to the one defined by Giorgio Agamben in his writing. See, Giorgio Agamben, Profanations (Cambridge: MIT Press, 2007).

The various accidents that jinx the project before and during construction do nothing but increase the heat. Groundbreaking is delayed a year as the city of Boston refused to grant building permits due to possible zoning violations. Hancock owns the adjacent property and swaps zoning credits; hearings and appeals drags on.

Permits are eventually granted only after Hancock threatens to move its headquarters to Chicago. During construction, the removal of large portion of earth and the effect of thousands (3,000) steel piles being driven into the bedrock, causes ground settling to occur effecting nearby Trinity Church, Sheraton Copley Plaza Hotel, streets, sidewalks and utility lines. Trinity experiences damage (cracking of transept walls) and sues.

Window installation—the largest windows ever to be installed in a tower (3.5 meter tall)—takes place in 1972 but throughout the fall a series of storms caused windows to break. By July 1973, almost half (2,472) of the window panes installed are shattered.[4] As a result, the building is cloaked in plywood, the architect is being reviled from one end of the land to the other. The project becomes the source of nation-wide jokes and innuendo, generating much tension around the Pei's firm, which see several other (good) clients go bring their business elsewhere.

4. Libbey-Owens-Ford, the glass manufacturer, eventually retested the strength of their glass. As a result, it was decided that all double-pane windows (10,344), half of which already installed, were to be replaced by ½ inch thick reflective tempered glass.

The investigation of the Hancock glass problem takes years,[5] but everything comes down to one decision point, namely when the architect is called upon (by the client) and ordered to reduce the size of the glazing, a move supposed to ensure safety, and to get the client off the hook. The smaller glass option is eventually not adopted thanks to highly hierarchical nature of US corporate culture, where one person, (the CEO) is in charge of making decisions about things affecting the image of the company.

The decision time comes at the building committee of the board where all executive unanimously recommended the glass be replaced with smaller glass pieces. That was my one and only opportunity, HNC recalls, to forestall that. I told them point blank: "If you build the building as it was designed, there is a chance that this building will be acknowledged as a good citizen. If you build the building with the subdivided glass, you, the John Hancock Company, will never be forgiven. After being show a dramatic rendering of what the building would look like with the glass subdivided, the CEO decides to overrule the board: "We are going to proceed with the building as designed."[6]

---

5. A group from MIT, led by Prof. Robert Hansen, placed 70 wind sensors in locations around the exterior to assess the building's conduct in the wind and constructed a mockup of the Tower and the surrounding area to process wind tunnel tests. Two 300 lbs. dampers were installed on the 58th floor to prevent sway. Zurich-based expert on tall buildings from the Swiss Federal Institute of Technology employed by Hancock at HNC's urging, persuaded Hancock to stiffen the steel skeleton by adding 1,650 tons of diagonal struts at a cost of 6 million dollar.

6. In a conversation with the author, HNC said the following: "Behind this decision was two years of the most intense relationship. I mean the worst nightmare of a relationship that you can have with a client, and I would say that

HNC's final design, unveiled on November 27, 1967, shows a strategy of minimalism not for ideological reasons, but because the situation imposed it. The extreme disparity in size between the tower and the church is the central predicament faced by the architect, who chooses to deal with it not by creating a gratuitous distance between the two but by bringing them into close proximity while positioning and shaping the tower at an angle so that the church becomes the autonomous center and the tower the contingent satellite in the composition.

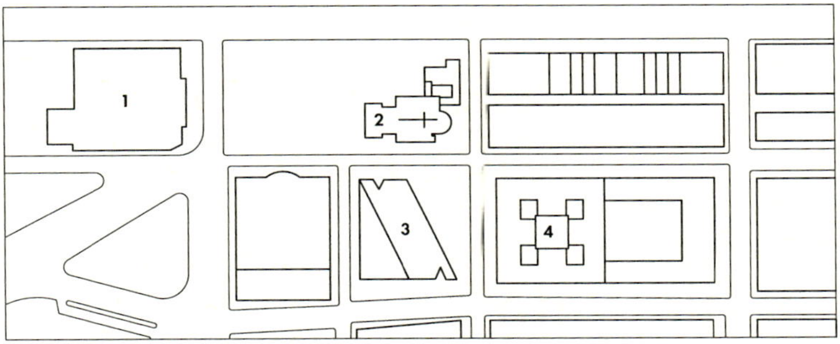

Site plan:
1. Boston Public Library;
2. Trinity Church;
3. John Hancock Tower;
4. Clarendon Building

---

the achievement that I am proudest of in my whole life it is that I conducted my relationship with that chairman in such a way that, when it came to that decision, he would overrule everybody else. That's the thing that I am most proud of in my whole life. I did that not by talking about my aesthetic concerns. I did that by convincing them that my interest was their only interest. The only reason it was accepted by this man is because we had built a relationship out of the most difficult circumstances over a period of two years in which he had a certain confidence that I would not say that out of self interest, that I would only say it out of concern for them."

The plan shows a parallelogram tower, a rhomboid planform the emphasizes the planar presences of the building and minimizes the volumetric one. Being placed diagonally, the rhomboid effectively disembodies the tower as seen from the square.

Two notches bisecting the end walls accentuate the weightless verticality of these planes and make the tower's nonrectangular geometry legible. The triangular space created between the church and the broad face of the tower set the stage for the apsidal view of the church, expanding the urban perception of Copley Square.[7]

Clad in glass, the building is designed to reflect the images of surrounding architecture. The tower's uniformly gridded and reflective surface, stripped of all elements that might suggest a third dimension, mutes the obtrusiveness of its enormous bulk and defers in all respects to the sculptural qualities of its much smaller neighbor. The architect believes that this is the option that will allow him 'to temper the inherent arrogance of so large a building and endow it with a presence that might animate rather than oppress the urban scene.' Even the three-story-high lobby at the base, the only 'public' part of the program is hidden away from outside perception.

"Had the monumental scale of this space been directly expressed or exposed to view from the outside," says HNC, "it surely would have upset the delicate balance in the dialogue between church and tower." The JHT stands alone

---

7. About the importance of in between spaces, one should recall Mies's words: "Modern buildings of our time are so huge that one must group them. Often the space between these buildings is as important as the buildings themselves."

on its (mutilated) feet. It remains resolute in its adherence to strict autism. A mute, opaque, impenetrable, silent and mysterious object dropped in the middle of Back Bay[8] that defies entry, being content to serve as the silent custodian/counterpart of the adjacent church. The high rise refuses to say anything to anyone other than reflecting the brutality of the XX century's impact on the city.

good citizens

"High-rises are by natural skeletal buildings. No noodles nor armored turrets. An arrangement of girders that carry the weight. Tall building consist of skin and bones." Mies van der Rohe's famous take on the high rise stems for his early 1920s Berlin competition entries. It is one of the few Mies's well-known (and praised) general statements that the JHT manages to mock by it sheer presence, which is reflecting not so much the neighboring structures by the HNC's heartfelt belief that general statement in architecture make little sense.

The JHT stands out as an indifferent, silent object. At a same time it is connected to Boston, to Copley Square and the set of circumstance that brought it into being. The JHT reflects in an extreme, hyperbolic matter the conflicts that are inherent in any buildings in general and in the TOB in particular. It reflects the conflict between the general—normally embodied by programs of use—and the

8. Back Bay is a Boston neighborhood famous for its rows of Victorian brownstone homes and considered one of the best preserved examples of XIX century urban design in the US.

specific—usually embodied by its art status. It also reflects the very status of architecture of being contaminated by the system of action that govern society: art, use, power. It is for this very reason that while being a mute object, the JHT say something about Boston in general and about the specific circumstance of the space surround Trinity Church as it has evolved throughout the centuries.

Prudential says nothing about Boston. It could be anywhere. The JHT is emblematic of Boston, Bostonians and their guilty consciousness, as Rudolf Arnheim put in its *Dynamic of Form*, published right after the JHT is completed.[9] Arnheim writes that the tower betrays its guilty consciousness, a statement HNC finds to be right on the money as he finds that the JHT "embodies a tragic view of history." The tower asserts its otherness, its separateness. Its alienation is explicit as it does not pretend to be a part of the culture that is embodied in the surrounding buildings. If tragedy is alienation and hopelessness, that the tower is tragic, as it expresses, in a poetic way, the impossibility of a reconciliation.

Neither function nor structure are given expression in the JHT. Both options are suppressed in favor of a completely contingent form. Indeed, what is impressive about it is how a pedantic, functionalistic office space arrangement in plan is hidden away by a curtain wall that leaves out no sign of what is happening inside of it. The JHT is also extremely careful and extremely indifferent to its immediate context and the life it takes place within it. The fundamental compactness of its primary, architectural form is utterly

---

9. Cfr. Rudolf Arnheim, The Dynamics of Architectural Form, 1978.

spectacular and unspectacular at the same time. Its sheer, enigmatic presence makes one forget all other features/ components of the event. It presents its visitors with a vast, imposing opaque vertical surface that welcomes no one. It is a solid mass of reflective glass that invites visitors to embark upon a peripatetic fruition of it, trying to accumulate a series of kinetic views of it. Ultimately though, the experience of the JHT relies in the irresolvable contradiction of its character, which is extremely functional and extremely formal at the same time. Its formal composition are autonomous and self-referential to the way the building is lived and used and make no attempt to hint about the spectacular static feast that the structure embodies.[10]

The paradox of a private, mute and impenetrable functionalist building becoming 'theatrical' by forcing participation upon the city dwellers cannot be argue in functionalistic terms: functionalist design is about designing easy to use/easy to understand space as the latter, so the rhetoric goes, designs itself just by following program and function. The paradox can perhaps be talked about only in terms of being 'contemporaneous' in an anachronistic fashion. In an odd, curious way, when considered from at larger (urban) scale, the JHT serves as a *campanile* to Trinity Church which managed to put back on the map Copley

---

10. Through these early structural failures, the JHT managed to play an important role in the history of building technology for its technological advances as the vision of the architects went beyond the era's technological capabilities. The JHT served as a lesson on how to install large glass plates in a high rise building, how to minimize sway in such a structure and was the case study that led to the development of additional testing procedures in the construction of high-rises.

Square, while the latter was threatened to become secondary and obsolete by Prudential Tower.

In this sense, the JHT plays an 'heroic' and courageous role in meeting, and winning, the challenge provided by Prudential by implementing Occam's razor hypothesis.[11] By appearing useless, or void of function, or sharing the so-called zero condition of a monument, it manages to 'profane'[12] what was considered a sacred, untouchable place by resorting to an anachronistic, primary object that helps us to understand the potential of architectural form and the role of the architect in expressing it. Here architectural form is understood as matter of courage, as courage is the necessary pre-requisite of being 'contemporaneous.' It means to be punctual at a meeting for which one cannot be late as it requires, to put it as Agamben did, "to be able to look in the face the darkness of our time and to be able to perceive, within the darkness, the light that, even if directed towards us, it keeps getting away from us."[13]

As a scion of one of first families to settle in the Boston area in the XVII century, a very much private human being, HNC proved to be able to raise to the challenge (acting in a fashion opposite to what everyone expected of him)

---

11. Occam's razor is a problem-solving principle devised by an English scholastic philosopher and theologian, William of Ockham. The principle states that among competing hypotheses that predict equally well, the one with the fewest assumptions should be selected. Other, more complicated solutions may ultimately prove to provide better predictions, but—in the absence of differences in predictive ability—the fewer assumptions that are made, the better.

12. The concept of profanation is here used in the sense defined by Giorgio Agamben in his Profanations (Cambridge: MIT Press, 2007).

13. Cfr. Giorgio Agamben, Che cosa è il contemporaneo? (Roma: Nottetempo, 2008).

showing that he was indeed equipped with such anachronistic sense of time and courage.[14] He understood his heritage as an obligation to engage with a bad client and his bad program because, precisely because of his status, he felt he had all the right cards up his sleeve to play the diplomatic game required to turn a bad client into a good citizen, the JHT itself and, by extension, architectural form itself, understood as a powerful negation of all general statements about form, function, context and their political correctness. The JHT embodies the perennial ambivalence of architectural form and of its silent presence.

---

14. HNC: "Sometimes, the architect's intentions are very close to the client's, and sometimes they're very far. My claim is that you can make good architecture or bad architecture out of either situation. I don't care how bad the client, I don't care what the situation is. As architects, we are responsible and only we are responsible. Whatever happens, whatever the circumstances, if the architecture is good—by good, I mean that it expands the perception and awareness of the public to whom it's addressed—then the architect deserves credit. If it isn't, then the architect, and only the architect, is responsible. That's my view. [I think it's very hard to generalize about almost anything in architecture. I do not know how to generalize about the kind of things that an architect should turn away from rather than engage in. The truth is that if I hadn't happened to have been born in Boston, born and brought up in Boston, if I hadn't happened to feel that I knew this scene so well that I was in a sense somewhat 'entitled' to make judgments about it, even though those judgments ran counter to the judgment of essentially all of my colleagues in the profession here, I certainly wouldn't have presumed to do it. I mean, I've built towers on five continents, and I would not do the JHT on any continent, in any city, except Boston. I would not presume to intrude in that way in a city. It was only because I believed that there was an opportunity there, and that I should seize it."

2019: Modernisms at 100

a personal wake

Berlin, 2019. Unpublished

The notes that follow are my own personal celebration of the Bauhaus's 100 year anniversary. The goal is to examine the past with an archeologist's frame of mind—following the famous psychoanalytical paradigm of the return of the removed—to attempt to enucleate the powerful parasites that have been dwelling inside the architectural 'debate' for over a century: the virulence of the hysterical optimism of the old and new fundamentalists of radical modernity who are unable to perceive what Hans Magnus Enzensberger called the 'puff pastry' of time. I call it archaeological investigation because it deals with both the onset point of the phenomenon and its most likely cultural source: the Prussian Protestantism of Martin Luther which was perhaps best described by Lichtenberger in the following manner: 'and like a scorpion he will spread the poison that has in its tail.' It is a line that suggests a method of inquiry worth pursuing when interrogating the genesis of modernism and its consequences.

In 2019 the 'engine' of Western cultural production is found to be increasingly idling, despite the deafening noise it keeps producing. One notices a drowsy driver circling round and round, intoxicated by the vapors of a nit-picking, bureaucratic world debilitated by ever more intrusive digital devices. Outside of the bureaucratic and digital, very little appears to be happening. There is no glimmer of transcendence or metaphysics. *La promesse de bonheure* with which Stendhal identified the character of beauty has lost its appeal, and the drowsy driver seems to be inhabiting a long night of short shadows. One by one, it is disabling almost all the figures and attributes that once had the purpose of rendering human lives livable. The intoxicating cultural engine has consequences for architecture as well: What cultural role can architectural form have today?

The question itself presupposes the fact that the relationship with architectural form has become problematic because the very meaning of form is now enveloped by a cloud of opacity. This is probably due to a century of demonization of a different kind. No one is surprised if a 2019 culture, which is unable to resist the power of anniversaries, is eager to celebrate 1919 as the year in which the world population was hit by the news of an almost supernatural event that was mesmerizing. However few were equipped to truly understand it.

Simply told, on the night of May 29, 1919, in a remote Brazilian village called Sobral, two scientists—Davidson and Crommelin—managed to take a picture of a solar eclipse. The snapshot proved the 'non-invalidity' of the theory of general relativity published by a German-born Jewish theoretical physicist called Albert Einstein, which inextricably linked space and time in a four-sided dimension. According to this watershed theory, gravity is nothing more than the manifestation of the curvature of space-time. Upon publication in 1915, the theory was met with skepticism by the scientific community because it was only derived from mathematical reasoning and rational analysis and not from experiments and observations. The 1919 solar eclipse wiped out the skepticism and proved to be instrumental in creating a much needed optimism to a world severely tried by the horrors of a world war. Einstein's name became world famous in a way that is unusual for a scientist. His name was immediately turned into a byword for genius. In the minds of many, the reason for his global fame is due to the timing of his appearance on the developing global stage of the era.

However as far as Germany is concerned, the year 1919 is also being celebrated for what has been presented, time and time again, as a similar watershed event for the world of architecture. They are celebrating the official opening of the *Staatliches Bauhaus on March 21, 1919* in Weimer, Germany. It was an offshoot of two Weimer schools—the School of Arts and Crafts and the College of Fine Arts—conceived of by its founding director, Walter Gropius. This educational *merger* has traditionally been presented as Gropius' main claim to fame, yet many believe that Gropius should be known for a different, notorious, yet truer fame: the despotic banning—preached for on a Transatlantic scale for the first time in history—of tradition from the mind of the architect who wanted to call himself 'modern.' In the words of one of his Harvard students, Henry Cobb, Gropius set in place 'what is perhaps the worst kind of tyranny: the tyranny that compels one to remain ignorant.' A judgment suggesting that the reason for Gropius 'fake fame' is also due to timing.

Thirty years ago, Aleksandre Kojève argued that after 1989 the *Homo sapiens* has been left with two alternative possibilities: behave in the post-historical animal fashion incarnated by the American lifestyle, or resort to the snobbism of the Japanese who keep celebrating ceremonies void of meaning. As an architect practicing in Europe, I shall like to think that there is a third option: confront our own past in order to gain a renewed energy to live and work. In this connection, one is perhaps best served by zooming back a century and considering the German context after World War I. In 2019, one cannot help but feel intrigued by the notion that an unconscious parasitic relationship with Modernism and the location of its 'cradle', namely the German-speaking Lutheran lands in which modernism came into being, is arguably responsible for many of its discontents.[1] In the mind of the present writer, the latter are mostly the consequence of a recklessness performed by the modern: substitute the two hinges around which architectural form revolve—figuration and the mystery of

---

1. The possibility of the existence of a toxic parasitic link between the inflexibility of modernist architects and Prussian Lutheranism was made evident to the present author the very second he moved to the capital of Prussian 'Zivilisation.' To most non-Prussian subjects, Berlin still appears in need of radical actions of civilization, even though this seems like a lost cause, or a project with no prospect of success whatsoever. As James Hawes expresses, this is because 'Prussia remains a country which, by most of the normal standard of European nationhood—history, geography, political arraignment, religion—are still entirely foreign. [...] Western Germany should stop wasting money trying to please a region (like Prussia) that will never be pleased.' Crf. James Hawes, *The Shortest History of Germany*, (New York: The experiment, 2017), a brilliant book that outlines *la longue durèe* of key, historically problematic issues hidden in German history that date back to Roman times and a millennia-long resistance to the Latin language and Christian-based values. The remarks about first hand exposure to the topic can be read in note 3 of the preliminary remarks and they apply here as well.

non-linear time—with a toxic proscription of guilt and fear of sin as a form of life.[2]

The time has come to confront some of the key words hit—like *la figura, il tempo, la morale*—or sneakily introduced—like *il peccato, la colpa*—by the unforgiving rhetorical train of the modern, against the contribution of three main protagonists of cultural history—Luther, Dante, Warburg—who can help us find the way to finally bury the modernist rhetoric once and for all. This has become urgent

---

2. The immediately apparent and remarkable aspect of the German mindframe is its unusual architecture, where 'rules' and life are two facets of one unbreakable coin: rules are not means but ends. In Germany, a rule is absorbed without leaving viable connections with life. This opens up the question: What is human life, if in its every gesture, every word, every silence, it can no longer be distinguished from the rule? Much like the Franciscans, Germans seem to be in need of living their life like an incessant and integral liturgy that becomes an *horologium vitae* that scans every moment of the time of life. It has been suggested by many that the origin of this form-of-life is Luther himself, as he somehow simultaneously sponsored an absolute abandonment of the believer in the hands of God and a radical refusal of the world which he painted as the kingdom of evil. It was a double action that prevented the shaping of any sense of free will or citizenship, which developed in neighbouring countries. The German version was rather a sense of passive obedience to all forms of authorities, as if, uncannily, their ruling was not to be questioned in any shape or form. A troubling consequences is that when a German individual becomes part of society, he blends in as a man-mass. He supinely adheres to the demands of the group. He forgets all the best values of his inner world, as if they belonged to someone else, or as if they had been forgotten at home. Cfr. Heinrich Mann, *The Subject*, a prophetic 1914 novel (published in 1918) that outlines the portrait of a 'perfect German subject' with crude and grotesque sarcasm. The subject is marked by the Prussian whippings from his father to his socio-political triumph. All the stages of his 'maturing' are outlined and punctuated with rhythmic ferocity: the dissipated student life, tragic drinking, shameful love affairs, military service, and taking responsibility of his father's company and his family.

because neglecting to confront the transformation of these words, which were induced by modernism, has ultimately triggered the process of progressively emptying essential architectural categories from within.

La Figura

For the greater part of twentieth-century, art and architecture was based on a negative kind of ideology fed by an iconoclastic attitude that sought to ban a good number of things in general, as well as any use of Images in particular. Much was outlawed: as the architectural form was hit by a moralistic attitude equipped with the power of deciding what was permissible or not. Anecdotes, narratives, literary associations, story lines, and references to tradition were left at the door of the avant-garde party room. The modern movement's messianic redemption made a clean sweep of any accumulation of the fundamental elements of a rich millennial discipline to reach a largely unattainable ideal: the truth of form beyond form itself.

Modern iconography called for neutral buildings that were the reflection of the 'modern' architect's disciplined and obedient transcription of the *zeitgeist* of an iconoclastic era. In the ideology of the modern, the architect's task was to simply implement a program of social redemption that left no room for discussion of architectural form and its autonomy. Those elements left the scene quietly. On the basis that architectural form could only be an illustration of a program or, at least, a direct expression of social purpose by fusing form and word—articulated as expression and content, system and concept, practice and theory—any notion of Image or iconographic references were solemnly condemned and effectively erased from the very core of architectural discourse. The result was that they were simply kicked out of the field of architectural debate as *personae non gratae*.

Today it seems that such purging was an attempt to substitute the ontological political realm of beauty with direct political action in order to actively belong to a new kind of new democratic society. The perspective seduced people like Ernst May and Hannes Meyer, whose choices and positions were later sanctified and became a real hypostasis for a social redemption that did not happen, obviously. What was also sacrificed in this sanctification, which has lasted for a 100 years, was *figuration*. In fact after 1919, people stopped producing reasoned arguments about figuration. To this day, neither the press nor academia even dares to mention the word 'beauty'. This is perhaps an index of the radicalism of this approach and its centenary success.

Yet in the XXI century, a new focused attention on figuration has resurfaced. This is happening exactly at a time when a sea of images are being produced daily by the vast majority of a population that is unable to resist the seductive power of all kinds of digital devices that keep inundating the public sphere. Those devises are producing a seemingly unstoppable stream of intimate images. The phenomenon is so pervasive that many wonder whether we now live inside of a global iconic cocoon from which we cannot escape. Most images are being produced for unfocused 'entertainment purposes' as a deluge. The deluge inherently carries the notion of impotency. To a certain extent in today's world, images are perceived and treated as the primary element of our public life, even though this has made a show of our intimate life.

However it would be childish to hide the unquestionable

success of the modern movement, or fail to understand it as a sort of historical necessity. In less than a decade, the nineteen twenties, modern architecture was brought to life after the end of the war by a number of 'midwives' working in the midst of formidable prejudices. The latter invested architectural form with a mantle of (modern) heroism that perhaps contributed to fog the mind of everyone involved on the battlefield, good guys and the bad guys alike. Modern architects fought tooth and nail to be accepted and then established.

Eventually, they become 'institutionalized' some two decades later in a different country all together, USA. However, it is arguably necessary to elaborate on its most tragic failure: iconoclastic tendencies. 'The true symbol of the modern age in architecture is the *absence* of visible symbols [...] we will tend to ask architecture itself to assume a lower degree of visibility,' wrote Mumford in 1940 in a then popular attempt to formulate the only acceptable *pedigree* for architectural form. For him, and many well-known others, architectural form was to be derived from the 'experience of the present' rather than the logic of its own tradition, or from its expressive autonomy. It is possible to suggest that the seeds of this view were first planted in the fashionable Bauhaus crowd.

Il tempo

One should considered the gulf between what was being promised in 1919 and what was actually delivered. In 2019, one finds that the Bauhaus was introduced as a sort of marketing brand. Perhaps as the first brand ever, in the architectural world at any rate. Its name, whose cleverness would remain as the only item destined to receive the perpetually hard-to-get appreciation of Mies van der Rohe. It refers to the medieval *Bauhütten*—a small and simple hut for builders. The brand itself—literally 'house building'—was meant and understood to mean 'School of Building.' However in spite of its name, its manifesto—which proclaimed that the aim of all creative activity was building—and the fact that its founder was an architect, the Bauhaus never managed to receive funding for a proper architecture department. In Gropius' mind, this might have been a metaphorical shelter from the elements, one backed by the government support and Weimer authorities. Yet their expectations, however, do not exactly match Gropius' radical intentions. He wanted to establish a new and unprecedented cultural path of millennial significance for the discipline of architecture that was heading towards nothing less than the creation of a new universal society for the 'new' man.

The school's goal was said to be the opposite of what Adolf Loos preached: to get the arts out of crafts. The Bauhaus' goal was in contrast, specifically breaking down of all sorts of barriers between the arts, arts and people, arts and crafts, and artists of different nations. Its mission was to bring everything related to the design world under one roof: painting, sculpture, architecture, furniture, applied arts and handicrafts. Its social message was unequivocal: art is not the playground of the privileged, and, in turn, it can be pursued by all those who intend and have the spiritual energy to do so.

There seems to be a consensus among the *cognoscenti* that the Bauhaus crowd had three utterly absurd aspirations. The first: to create a *Gesamtkunstwerk*—a total work of Art—in which all Arts, including architecture, would eventually be brought together. The second: to be in sync with the *zeitgeist*—the spirit of the time—thus kicking out any notion of space being central to any architectural discourse all together. The third: to annihilate the study of history and historical precedent because the *Stunde Nulle*—the zero hour—had struck. The clock of Time was to be reset and deserved a fresh start in which 'real time' had to be given precedence to any non-linear sense of time, like, for instance, such as the sense of timelessness stemming from figuration or the mystery of beauty.[3]

A popular European saying states that Germany, having created a global state a war twice in the span of a quarter century, 'brought back the clock of history a hundred years.' One wonders if the same applies to the Bauhaus. Did it push back the clock of history a hundred years? In 2019, it is certainly impossible not to see the ambition of the school, and modernism, by extension: replace tradition with the arrogance of sponsoring one-self as being the person elected to address the future. And that this was obtained by resorting to an 'objective,' pseudo-scientific aestheticization of society based on the 'dataification' of it. In other words, the notion that 'design,' in all its forms, could have but one goal: change society in order to design a society in sync with the obsession of modernism being one with 'real time.' In most cases, the expulsion of figuration was the consequence of a computational paradigm according to which anything that cannot be 'calculated' did not have the right of citizenship in the modern citadel.[4]

---

3. For a stark critique of the linearity of time introduced by the modern, the reader should refer to the remarks in note 4 of the preliminary remarks. They apply here as well.

4. Mutatis mutandis, it is not difficult to see the same obsession in the Dutch

Datafication seems unstoppable nowadays as we find ourselves in the process of experiencing the emergence of social structures, mindsets and ways of life that are simply inconceivable without it. Data-based processes in which places and objects are encoded, trans-coded and re-coded lead us to a world that is no longer based on traditional knowledge. The collection and utilization of data forms the new basis of society.

La morale

A century ago, a new figure emerged in the European context: the figure of the architect as a sort of a 'scientific' liberator of mankind's most ancient troubling areas of thought or intellectual preoccupation—like the never easy engagement with symbolic content or pure beauty itself—as the result of a synthetic approach. Yet, as it became prominently evident after the Transatlantic crossing, the utopian stance of modern architecture, the ambition to be able to design and shape a *radiant town*—a town where life would be simultaneously intelligent, healthy and educative, thriving on social justice and political fairness—was ostensibly not part of the American landscape. In his introduction to five 'Germanic' architects affected by a misguided, almost frivolous nostalgia for the glorious 1920s, Colin Rowe acutely (but not entirely accurately) pointed out that a number of significant adjustments occurred on the

---

speculation of the last 25 years. To be considered cool, buildings have to be a sort of literal transposition of a large number of 'data' their architects deem 'valid' because they are derived from the program.

modernist's architectural stance during its Transatlantic crossing.[5] The most significant one was the exclusive emphasis on its supposedly glorious, mythical body—*la physique*—at the expense of its political message—*la morale*—which so greatly characterized its 1920s German-built cradle of architecture. The latter experienced a significant cultural shift once deported to the USA. That shift's true significance has not been object of much critical scrutiny. Basically, the impeccably 'good intentions' of the Lutheran approach failed to be packed in the suitcases of those architects who managed to cross the ocean. *La morale*, on the contrary, had no trouble whatsoever in changing its 'clothes' and forgetting any notion of posing a challenge to the social order by proposing radical social reconstruction. The good intentions quickly became a new approach to building or, as famously put by Rowe himself, *decor de la vie* for Greenwich, Connecticut. It was an approach that made modernism 'safe' for American capitalism.

Yet herein lies the rub, one which has a direct bearing on the present day. The time has come to give things their proper name in an attempt to dispel the confusion. If it is true that the Marxist aura and ambition of the revolutionary *avant-guarde* quietly left the scene, all other facets of its Lutheran rhetoric not only remained but also resonated particularly well with the Puritan transcendentalism that has generally characterized American soil since its

---

5. The built work of the (culturally speaking) five 'Germanic' men with American passports introduced by Rowe in 1972 appear very often, as aptly suggested by Rowe himself in the postscript, an 'excuse for producing drawing rather than a case of producing drawing as an excuse for building.' Cfr. *Five Architects*, curated by Arthur Drexler, New York: MoMA, 1972.

inception and the *Alma Mater* of modernism in America, in particular.[6]

In this light, it is possible to admit that it was not correct to suggest, as Rowe did, that what was discarded was *la morale* (and all the escapists myths attached to it) 'for the benefit of the *physique* as the only useful and usable member of the overall modernist stance because of its eloquence and overwhelming flexibility as derived by the plastic and spatial inventions of cubism and constructivism.'

What was truly discarded was *la politique*, not *la morale*. In contrast, *la morale* proved to be a potent vehicle for the promotion and development of a modernism which was politically indifferent yet morally active. This is a crucial role that has been strangely overlooked by most critics, both 'operative' and historical. This might be because the majority of them were brought up in a Protestant environment.[7]

While the political agenda was surgically removed from the intellectual table, the religious Lutheran tone was not. Most of its basic misunderstandings and widely accepted condemnations remained attached not only to modern architecture but also to architectural debate *tout court*.

---

6. Here the reader is referred to another piece collected in the present anthology: Modernism in America: the Harvard job.

7. A quick list of English-speaking sponsors or critical voices about modernism would include, in no particular order, Kaufmann, Greenberg, Rowe, Banham, Gedion, Pevsner, Vidler and Frampton. Interestingly enough, even Italian speaking critics, like Ciucci, Tafuri, Dal Co, Benevolo, Portoghesi, Zevi and many more failed to make the argument, perhaps because they were unfamiliar with Protestant lifestyles (with the exception of Zevi).

In the 1990s, I had a series of conversations with Henry N. Cobb revolving around his professional life. He had been deeply entangled, for personal and historic reasons, by the particular brand of Transcendental Modernism sponsored by Harvard University under Gropius, who ran the school during his time as a student there. Differently from the Weimer years, Gropius was actually in charge of running a proper architecture school in USA. His Bauhaus pedagogical model, which was never implemented in the city of Weimer in Germany, is therefore best understood when approached from that experience.

As a Harvard student in the late 1940s, Cobb thought that Gropius' educational program was fairly explicit in one aspect: the idea that architecture should attack important and difficult problems in society and culture. 'In those days though, the word culture was never used; it was social problems that architecture should address!' According to Cobb, there was little else in terms of positive thinking. 'I think projects were certainly judged in formal terms but much of the criticism was—both in the studio and in reviews—was on a level so blatantly functional as to be really boring, I guess, plain boring. We used to make jokes about it but the fact is that it is true that some critics were only interested in back-to-back plumbing: if you put your toilets back-to-back, the project is OK; if they're not back-to-back, you fail, you know, it was that kind of thing. What does this reflect? It reflects an absence of any kind of theoretical or formal structure or ideology on the part of the faculty. Everybody was at sea, I would say.'

Speaking about his thesis, a group of residential towers for the Boston harbor, Cobb still thinks that it reflected the worrisome void at the very center of the Harvard pedagogy set by Gropius. 'At Harvard,' Cobb reported, 'Gropius was implementing the so-called basic design program he had envisioned, but never implemented, at the Bauhaus because the Bauhaus never managed to fund a proper architecture department. The problem with that program was that, while it was based on the idea that architecture was now liberated from the tyranny of dead styles. But beyond the affirmation of that liberation there was alarmingly little substance or coherence. There was, in my view, an absence of the kind of discipline that is the traditional precursor of achieving mastery of in any field. In other words, there was no coherent program of training.'

In hindsight, it is so ironic that in its first international move, Harvard invited a surprising individual to work in the country. That person turned out to be, culturally speaking, an isolationist. According to many witnesses, this was a person who reduced architecture to instrumental training that was intolerant of many things, including history. Cobb found him directly responsible for 'a lot of the follies of architectural education that, if we are honest, emerged not so much from espousing one point of view over another but from the intolerance that is engendered by the intolerance of other. The idea that Gropius thought that students were not even allowed to think about certain things.'

Architects from Cobb's generation who studied under Mies described the general atmosphere at the schools as puritanical. Kevin Roche said that one was constantly in fear of sin, as Mies had really created the idea of mortal sin in architecture and, above all, the idea that there was a right way to do something, and there was a wrong way. In hindsight, it can be said that the tyranny of the Mies school was a tyranny of a training style, a kind of discipline that one was obliged to undergo. However, it assumed that, after absorbing this discipline and training, the gifted ones would then use it as the basis for inventing one's own architecture and the less gifted would at least do less harm, because they would work with a certain discipline in mind. In other words, the premise of the *Ecole des Beaux-Arts*. To put it another way, a permanent fear of sinning as a form of life had accompanied modernism since the very beginning, as if building was a sort of monastic rule blurring into life itself. It was a rule with obsessive attention paid to the proper interpretation of time which overwhelmed any consideration about the facets that are fundamental to comprehend architectural form in the end. An example is its *Voluptas*, ne made of sensual lyricism.

La colpa

The remarkable thing about the Berlin architectural scene is that, in spite of an enormous volume of construction implemented at a frantic pace in the last quarter of a century, it remains a scene of limited cultural interest or ambition. One question has been in the air for a quarter of a century: 'Why is German architecture so subaltern?' Why is it always perceived as well-detailed but boring? In 1993 Dieter Hoffmann-Axthelm thought that this was due to a 'lack of expression,' derived from the Nazi trauma that left German architects speechless.

In a 2012 article entitled 'Normal at Last? New German Architecture Off the Therapist's Couch,' Anh-Linh Ngo justified the post-war longing for normality as a consequence of architecture's entanglement with the Nazi regime, even though such entanglement, if compared to other regimes like the Italian pre-war regime, for example, had been truly insignificant in terms of built structures since it actually never managed to leave the drawing board for real. The author went on to wish for a new 'normalcy' in architectural form which would finally be able to become an 'agent' in the structuring of social relationships, because apparently, in his opinion, it was exactly what German architects had been fearing because of the Nazi trauma. The thesis confirms one inconvenient truth. People who never practiced architecture in Berlin are ill-suited to acknowledge the evidence produced by practice, namely that the cultural proximity between the culture of moral demonization and fear revolving around the rhetoric of the Bauhaus and the *Baupolizei*—as the current *Bauprufrung* (building inspectorate) was once called in Berlin (as the architect practicing in Berlin is forced to learn rather quickly)—is a more likely and logical culprit.[8]

To practice architecture in Berlin is, in fact, to familiarize oneself with a seemingly endless list of *verboten* actions that invest what most other cultures would consider negligible. Most design decisions allowed outside of Germany are not even considered in Berlin. On top of that, the architect is personally liable for design *mistakes* for 30 years.[9] Yet, the architect familiar with less negative men-

---

8. Cfr. Bruno Taut, *Bauen. Der neue Wohnbau* (Berlin: Biermann, 1927) a text half-jokingly dedicated by the author to the 'dear Baupolizei' to justify the existence of the Berlin Ring of architects. The book is a resistance piece against the police-like method of Ludwig Hoffmann, a sort of German counterpart to Marcello Piacentini, who blocked almost every architectural endeavour that looked suspiciously 'contemporary.'

9. If the architect dies, his relatives are held responsible. This holds true for the thirty years following the design.

tal landscapes is struck by the extent with which German culture, in order to achieve an orderly (read: safe) human landscape, knows no alternative but forcing people to live in a permanent state of fear of being charged as a 'guilty sinner,' as if it were a judgment with no possibility of reconsideration. The public authorities still seem to particularly enjoy the sadism embedded in the act of making people's lives miserable (for incredibly insignificant reasons most of the time) by implementing a technique of psychological harassment that appears to be a derivative of the infamous, diabolical Stasi technique known as *Zersetzung*.[10]

Encumbered and oppressed by an unbelievable amount of liabilities, it is no wonder that Berlin's architects have traditionally shown (and continue to show) no enthusiasm for being intellectually 'daring' or experimental. They know too well the fake accusation that people love to charge them with at every turn. It is therefore not surprising that the Bauhaus rhetoric of negativity—*Thou Shall Not*—may be described for what it truly is: a historical consequence of a

---

10. In the words of the historian Hubertus Knabe: 'the Stasi used a diabolic technique called *Zersetzung*, which means "biodegradation," which is in fact an accurate description of its goal: to sublimirally destroy the self-confidence of people, for example by damaging their reputation, (like organizing failures in their work) and by destroying their personal relationships. In this light, East Germany was a modern dictatorship. The Stasi didn't try to arrest every dissident. It preferred to paralyze them, and it could do so because it had access to so much personal information and to so many institutions.' And of course, it needs to be remembered that the great advantage of perpetrating this sort of harassment was its subtle nature, which made it an almost textbook case for plausible deniability. As an architect working in Berlin, after having practices in the USA and Italy, I can only offer the personal impression of being forced to submit to a similar harassment, one that non-German cultures would find intolerable.

Kultur and *Zivilisation* (like the German one) which to this day is profoundly marked by a deviated Lutheranism that is ultimately responsible for having boxed people inside an inhuman, if not anti-human, mental cage of negativity.

Luther's job

One must admit: to rhetorically promote the modern stance, it was necessary to invest the whole argument with religious overtones, in order to individuate a heresy against which one could impose an orthodoxy of the messianic kind: the promise of a better world that can solely be achieved by resorting to the proper (scientific) use of architectural form. Ineluctable change was seen as a vehicle in order to avoid imminent catastrophes of the apocalyptic kind.

In hindsight the strategy appears derivative of what Martin Luther envisioned four centuries earlier when he established a mental landscape of fear that insured a high volume of believers. To accomplish that, Luther introduced the Bible as nothing less than the printed *Word of God*: the *only* reliable guide for faith. He believed that every passage of Scripture had one single, straightforward meaning. His key doctrine was a justification: humans are saved from their sins by God's grace alone (*Sola Gratia*), through faith alone (*Sola Fide*), and on the basis of Scripture alone (*Sola Scriptura*). Lutheran theology holds that God made the world, including humanity, holy and sinless. However, Adam and Eve chose to disobey God because they trusted in their own strength, knowledge and wisdom. Due to this, all humanity deserves eternal damnation in hell. Given the radicalism of such an messianic framework, it is not surprising that the figurative became the principal battlefield in the clash between Protestants and Catholics. According to Luther, the representation of the sacred constituted instrumental and inadmissible abuse. For the Roman Church, on the contrary, art was an ideal means of evangelizing the masses. Art was the best medium for the representation of the evangelical episodes because of the power of its figuration.[11]

Indeed, the question of images is where the gulf between Protestants and Catholics is measured The controversy began in 1522 when Andreas Bodestein von Karlstadt spread the notion that the cult of images was both a means of controlling the masses and a form of idolatry. As a product that was independent of the Holy Texts, which were considered the only repositories of divine revelation, art was viewed as an abuse of man carried out by the Church of Rome. This is how a violent campaign of destruction of icons and religious images began in Wittenberg, in the heart of the Protestant revolt, and eventually spread to Zurich, Nuremberg and Strasbourg.

Erasmus of Rotterdam sought to establish distinctions between the good and bad use of images and implicitly admitted that one can strike the soul of the faithful through sight. It is especially effective in penetrating those people who are less cultured, and it is much more effective

---

11. Luther, an Augustinian monk, produced a profound revision of the fundamental doctrines of the church, thus lighting the fuse of a vast political and religious rebellion in which the peasants rebelled against their lords. Fearing for the fate of his reform action, Luther harshly condemned the rebels, inciting the lords to exterminate the peasants by any means. The extermination allowed for the authoritarian German feudal structure to endure, unlike what happened in the Netherlands, France or the UK.

in reaching people than reading or listening. Condemning what was considered pure and simple superstition (the cult of the saints, which has no basis in the Holy Scriptures), the illustration of Christ's life was allowed instead, provided it was accompanied by an evangelical explanation. Zwingli firmly rejected any use of images in sacred and private spaces. This soon became particularly intransigent, since those images could only be impure by definition since they were a product of mankind.

During those years, the Protestant movements therefore tended to create an ever deeper gap between the word and image. The Catholic Church countered with the Council of Trent (1563), which reaffirmed the absolute necessity of the mediation of the priesthood and the intercession of the saints between God and the faithful. Approved by theologians, its final decree reaffirmed that the cult of images was to be considered a 'lawful' ideal means of addressing devotion by virtue of the communicative universality of the images themselves.

Thus one observation is clear: the Tridentine Church considered the translation of the divine into images as essential. As Paleotti put it: the task of art was 'to give a face to faith.' This was possible by purging the real from what is indecorous to alternatively promote what is effective value and realistic coherence (the *vero-simile* expressed in the formula 'image and similarity'). The painter's aim must be to persuade the public: 'to delight, to teach, to move to affection.' Even though there might be the need to underline that making the users of architectural form 'delight' or 'move to affection' was not exactly high on the itemized list that modernism deemed as important in order to practice architecture. On the contrary, those aspects were actually ostensibly absent.

An inconvenient truth is often underplayed, if not outright overlooked. Upon final analysis, the liturgy of the Catholic church is the embodiment of a mystery. It should not be understood as a secret doctrine, but rather a theatrical performance (a praxis) consisting of a number of ritualistic gestures performed through time for the salvation of mankind. Rather than referring to eternal truths that can be revealed or explained, the *Cristianesimo* is about implementing a liturgical theatrical action, whose main actors are Christ and the Church itself, in all its various memberships.

In this connection, it helps to reconsider one important fact: the invention of *Purgatorium*. It is not a very popular topic today. Instead, it can be considered a hot potato in the dispute between Protestants and Catholics. Luther called it the 'third place,' to suggest that it was a ridiculous XII century invention that was not included in the Scriptures. Yet, *Purgatorium* had been one of the most crucial notions in the evolution of Culture in Europe, as explained by Jacques Le Goff in a memorable book tracing its history.

The invention of *Purgatorium*, in fact, altered the geographical and mental horizon of the *Nachleben* of a society, like the Medieval society, which was impregnated and ruled by religion. Purgatory generated a new in-between spatiality and radically altered the fabric of time, introducing a time of hope and a latent but potent interaction between the dead and the living, who are supposed to help the dead in order to reach the destination that the very existence of Purgatory presupposes: the space of eternal salvation. But it is important to underline that the literary consequences of the invention of Purgatory. It is a *status* rather than a place, and its success is due to the iconography designed by Dante. By describing it, a landscape managed to turn popular credos into a seductive polyphony of images.

Schlegel considered Dante the first modern poet because Dante fused poetry and Christianity thanks to the extraordinary reservoir of images contained in the Divine Comedy. In fact, Dante understood the multidimensionality of Purgatory and its role as an intermediary: a spatial reification capable of connecting cosmology and theology. Purgatory is not buried in *La Divina Commedia*. It is a mountain located in the middle of the ocean. It consists of seven telescopic circles meant to purge the seven capital vices. The mountain leads to the star-studded sky. Purgatory is not a neutral place: it is a one-way place. Purgatory leads from Hell to Heaven. Its inhabitants 'sing with one voice,' as they do at funerals on the way to the cemetery after the coffin leaves the church. Ascension is the fundamental action performed by its temporary inhabitants. Venial sins are absent. Only capital ones must be atoned for. Purgatory is a kind of temporary Hell that evolves slowly and contrasts with the immutability of Hell.

Dante transformed the nature of Purgatory by making it a place of hope rather than damnation, thus confirming the twelfth-century theological vision that focused on penance. Hope is expressed in the act of praying, and the image of praying for the dead introduces the liturgical act as the key act, or the hinge around which all artistic activity to follow would revolve. The images invite prayer as an act of faith. The act of praying re-establishes a bond between the living and the dead as they pray together, even though they live in distant places. In the Comedy, life in Purgatory evolved according to a specific time frame. The formulation of Purgatory as a provisional 'third place' unhinged the very notion of immutable eternal time. Its formulation presented the suggestion that everything is subject to change or evolution.

The formulation of Purgatory, therefore, triggered enormous consequences on the relationship between images: their seductive and dynamic power, and their consequent, inevitable interaction with the world of art and architectural form. Creating Purgatory as an interim 'third place' actually unhinged the very notion of time as being identified by a single unchanging status. Upon final analysis, the suggestion was brought to the table that nothing is set in stone, and that everything, on the contrary, is subject to change or evolution. But it also clarified that a *Zeitfrage* (the question of the interaction between art and time) stands at the very centre of every artistic endeavour.

Warburg's job

An unusually daring argument, one that would arguably have pleased Vico,[12] can thus arguably be made: the way Dante described *Purgatorium* can perhaps be understood today as the planting of the seed of the theory of *Nachleben* (survival, afterlife) or the theory of the dynamic power of images in constant movement through time put together by Aby Warburg six centuries after Dante. This can be argued because Warburg's theory revolved around a dynamic but clearly identified cluster, a cluster made of all the

---

12. Here I am referring to Vico's fantasia as the operative tool required to bring life to the otherwise dry and lifeless 'bones of the past.'

very items that the modernist agenda strived to annihilate: memory, desire, energy, pathos, immemorial time, and time without time. Somewhat paradoxically, that idea of time revolved around one conceptual hinge: the fact that time stands at the very center of intellectual speculation about the arts, all arts, architecture included. Considering this theory, in fact, time is the medium through which the energy of the pathos of images is being driven *behind* the back of fake chronologies, or notion of time based on directionality (embodied by an arrow) or geometric figures (embodied by the circle of time).

'The history of art,' said Warburg, 'is a history of the transformation of figures, not of fake chronologies or absurd theory of justification.' He said this to explain his own fascination (shared by the present writer) for the fantastic aesthetic world of the first German Romantics. It was more specifically the artistic world that they created since they had been deprived of the pleasure of Purgatory by Luther, and, not surprisingly, they were in need of an alternative dream. This was a world filled with crucial aesthetic categories that are now banned, such as the *Witz*, the arabesque, the power of the fragment, and, last but not least, the *je-ne-sais-quoi*. [13] The time that is of interest here, and that Warburg was interested in, is the time populated by ruins and survival (that Warburg called *Nachleben*) that shaped time itself, as seen throughout history. It is a time that is simultaneously the self-organization of natural phenomena and the ordering of socio-historical events,

13. For a discussion of these categories, cfr. conrad-bercah, *berlin transfert, an atlas of aesthetic ideas* (Siracusa: LetteraVentidue Edizioni, 2021).

the awareness of the flow of *chronos,* and the thought of its *Nachleben*, as well as the founding place of memory. Hence, the fundamental retroactive action expected to be performed by images due to their immanent energy is the following: renew 'ancient' formal problems in order to formulate new proactive (read: contemporary) questions regarding architectural form as it evolves over time while being indifferent to the chronological order of time.

Contrary to the Modernist stance, but during the same time frame (1919-1929), Warburg understood the importance of not mutilating the human body and mind from images, like the invention of *Purgatorium* appears to be confirming, today more than ever. But the Warburghian position is of interest for architectural form because it underlines the importance of the mutual exchange of *pathos* between the many temporalities that shape architectural form. Architecture continues to maintain the one option that the modern wanted to negate: it can only continue to interact by involving ancient formulas of *pathos*. In other words, images are not inanimate objects, but *aliti di vento* in continuous transformation. They are a breath, a chemical solution of time and images fused together. In this sense, it is possible to envision the image of the architect, inherent in his theories, as a diver (armed with few certainties) who is perpetually moving on the bottom of the sea in search of enigmas to investigate. He has no ambition to solve them. The architect is a diver who has understood that he is immersed in a fluid made of time, in which all the beings of the past have been shipwrecked, and whose bodies continue to transform themselves as they are shaped by the fluid of time. Sometimes they have become corals and sometimes, into pearls. This is the field of application of a 'science without a name,' a science of time and history through which it is possible to be shaped by the observation of images as if they were reserves of historical material charged with time and intensified energy. Creatures, not objects, charged with *pathos*, where the term does not indicate suffering but the substantial character of form itself. A *pathos* full of potentiality ready to be set in motion, ready to be released. An anachronistic *pathos*, unhinged by the flow of time, which is not a representation, but a meeting point of spirits or ghosts, entangled in a mutual perennial dance that they themselves cannot abandon.

A personal Wake

The modern has been pronounced 'dead' a number of times, most notably by Charles Jencks. He believed that the hour of passing took place at 3:32 p.m. on July 15, 1972, when the first building of the infamous Pruitt-Igoe housing estate in St. Louis, Missouri, received the *coup de grace* by dynamite. It was later a view championed by Peter Blake and Tom Wolfe. But the reality is that modernism is still very much alive, and it can only stop poisoning the intellectual wells as a consequence of one important stance: once architects find the honesty to agree on calling out its various intellectual 'bluffs.'

In a traditional society, there is an absolute identity between the act of transmission and its content. When tradition loses its ability to transmit its life force, by extension, the system has to be broken. The modern movement can therefore probably be described as the consequence of a radical temporal difference that occurred at a juncture in history when it was necessary to invent and consequently legitimize a new authority. Despite this and because of the great technical and social changes in the early 1900s, the definitive implosion of the old authority made evident the fact that a tradition had been completely emptied of its content and its forms were roaming around like ghosts without a body or soul. The modern movement replaced tradition with iconographic shock, and loud, fast messages meant to mobilize the masses. In retrospect, this desire is understandable: it was impossible to metabolize the many changes taking place in such a short period of time. The evident bewilderment and horror of the First World War had led to despair.

Nonetheless, in light of the above, it would be childish to negate the Lutheranism of the tone with which modernism was brought to life. A tone that is perhaps responsible for two colossal mistakes that cost dearly for all architects: (1) to confuse the historical need to break with tradition versus the loss of tradition itself; (2) to have formed a toxic obsession about chronological time at the expense of space, thus failing to understand that the Kantian formal categories of Time and Space, as showed by the 1919 eclipse, can only be inextricably intertwined in a *Spiegelspiel* (a game of mirrors) which is constantly reflecting the mutual interaction of non-measurable dimensions: involuntary memory, non-linear time, and its permanent, mysterious renewal (re-appropriation) through the *Nachleben.*

Modernism in American: the Harvard job

Published in west workroom, Milan: Charta, 2007

Secularization is considered one of the salient features of modernity. For some, it designates a positive process of emancipation, while for others, a degenerative process of de-sacralization that opens the way to nihilism. Max Weber described it as 'disenchantment with the world,' a label that stuck. Entered into legal parlance during the Peace of Westphalia (1648) for the purpose of indicating the transfer of property from the Church to civil possessors, the term has come to indicate the process of progressive autonomy of institutions from the control and influence of the Church. A typical example would be the evolution of an institution like Harvard University from a predominantly religious institution into a secular one (with a divinity school now housing the religious element, illustrating differentiation). This piece suggests a different view.

However indirectly, this note critiques contemporary issues about modernism, architectural education, and Harvard University. It was written in New York in 1998 in response to T. S. Eliot's poignant observation that: "No culture has appeared or developed except together with a religion; according to the point of view of the observer, the culture will appear to be the product of the religion, or the religion the product of the culture." The purpose of writing it was not, as it may appear, to outline a definitive definition of a cultural phenomenon as complex as modernism. Nor was it intended to become a vehicle for observations on a variety of topics. The aim is to help to define the role of a school in the instalment and the evolution of the phenomenon of modernism. Having received my architectural education at Harvard half a century later, I felt entitled to explore its contribution, which, just like a doctrine, needs to be defined after the appearance of some heresy.

Regardless of their convictions, believers are characterized by one indisputable fact: their attraction to one, all-embracing idea or belief system. Ardent believers are usually the most needy, as they seem to crave a dogma in which everything genuine eventually fits—a complete system capable of embracing the morality and hopes of humankind and the past and future history of the universe, a system that can help them deal with human affairs. There are believers who sustain the existence of a superior being and those who contemplate various purposes for human existence, such as the pursuit of happiness or the possibility of transcendentalism—a philosophy that asserts the primacy of the spiritual and transcendental over the material and empirical. Transcendentalism was, in fact, one of the most important (self-defining?) cultural movements in the United States, and one may speculate that it may also have paved the way (via Harvard University) to another cultural movement: modernism. What follows is an attempt to define a school's role in shaping cultural phenomenon.

My notes register that transcendentalism was more of a movement than a sharply-defined school, that it was not a prerogative of intellectuals, and that its main purpose was actually to rule out intellectual inquiry. That it included everyone involved in shaping the then newly established country: businessmen, women, artisans, journeymen, farmers, men of the sea, sea captains, ministers, spinsters, in brief, everyone populating the land. That some men of letters, however, are believed to have played a more important role in its definition. That Emerson and Thoreau are usually identified as the most prominent members of the movement, which also influenced Longfellow, Hawthorne, and two New Yorkers, Herman Melville and Walt Whitman, the major poet of mystical + pantheistic individualism. That transcendentalism was not just a movement but a way of life, that it was based in New England, and that it radiated from the town of Concord, which, paradoxically, was America's first intellectual community. That it began to develop in the 1830s and flourished for a quarter of a century thereafter. That it marked a turning point in American thought, shifting it toward an anti-institutional individualism and that, although it was presented as something entirely new, it may have had intellectual roots in mystical speculations of different sorts, be they Hindu pantheism or Neoplatonism. That it was a reaction to eighteenth-century rationalism, Unitarianism, and, in various ways, to the psychology of Locke, even if his political doctrines—which simultaneously stressed the worship of property, the need for a division of powers, and the injustice of primogeniture, which is to say, the basis of the American way of life in contrast to traditional European principles of hereditary and aristocratic privilege—found their way inside the American Constitution and are still at work whenever a dispute between the President and Congress arises. That Locke's ethical doctrines may have had a role in defining the movement. That transcendentalism made Puritanism—the credo of the land—its own; that it inherited it, as evident in the way in which it influenced the work of all its authors, its bearded 'Bardi' and novelists. That one of the movement's central doctrines was God's immanence in the universe, as Emerson seems to imply in suggesting that every human being in their own aloofness represents a minuscule universe. That the ethics of *Thou Shalt Not* was another. That, thanks to way in which it came to be, the new land of America had been spared from European imperfection + corruption.

Ralph Waldo Emerson (1803-1882) stands out as the movement's most illustrious member. His life is interesting. He was born in Boston and educated at the Harvard Divinity School. As the son, grandson, and great-grandson of Protestant ministers, Emerson inevitably became a pastor of a Unitarian church. That was in 1829, the year he also married. Two years later, after the deaths of his wife and his brothers, he lost his faith and, subsequently, his ministry. In the throes of an acute spiritual crisis, his set sail, in 1831, for London. Unlike the Pilgrims who left Old England to settle in what, despite their longing to be master-less, they curiously called New England, Emerson's sought to become a disciple of the most prominent masters of the day: Coleridge, Carlyle, and Wordsworth. When he felt he had achieved this goal, he crossed the Atlantic back, traveling westward. Upon his return to Boston, he published *Nature*—transcendentalism's strongest manifesto—and began to spend time traveling and lecturing, replacing the pulpit with the lectern. He became the most sought-after speaker in the nation, winning national recognition and international fame. Nietzsche himself felt very close to Emerson and once stated that he could not praise him on the grounds that it would be like praising himself—an undeliverable *apologia pro vita sua per interposta persona*. Coming from the philosopher who stressed the inevitable (and continuous) return of the equal, who valued the needs of great men at the expense of the remaining bulk of humanity and whose views have since been adopted to justify the abandonment of democracy, this must sound paradoxical to anyone who has been educated to identify Emerson's doctrines as the touchstone of democratic endeavors. It is a curious historical coincidence or, in a somewhat musical fashion, almost an irony of history! Emerson, in any event, lived most his life in Concord, the hometown of Henry David Thoreau (1817-1862), the proud Harvard-bred inhabitant of the solitary cabin on the shores of Walden Pond, the surrounding woods of which are said to have provided the material for both his house and his revelations—*Thou Shalt Not* and its attached holiness, arguably the most self-imposed liberties of the then new land.

I mention all of this because it may just be that modernism or, at least, Harvard's version of it, was a cultural movement of comparable importance—a sharply-defined spiritual school that eventually became a movement. From the notes I felt compelled to take on modernism, it seems that the movement was abruptly, almost surgically, implanted in the United States in the 1930s, a century after transcendentalism. It, too, flourished for a quarter of a century, from 1938 to 1963,[1*] and by curious historical coincidence two out of three of the main 'ministers' of American modernism—Walter Gropius and Marcel Breuer—also spent a great deal of time in the Concord area, where, for a time at least, they themselves lived apparently *in concordia*. The white, pure and pristine, modern wood houses they designed together are said to have established a different kind of community, one which was an object of worship rather than a subject of conversation. The reading of modernistic manifestos leads one to believe that modernism, too, made puritan prudery its own. Though modernism was born in a different place and time and on a different continent altogether, it may be that once imported to America this modernism—this pure vehicle of the spirit of the time—might have inherited the spirit of the place to which it had been brought. This spirit was an almost direct offspring of the value system of the Pilgrims, who, having traditionally held the arts responsible for distracting men from the business of salvation, quite inevitably attached to the practice of architecture the necessity of many renunciations, the main theme of Thoreau's life, namely, *Thou Shalt Not Have Aesthetic Enjoyment*. According to Emerson, Thoreau "was bred to no profession; he never married; he lived alone: he never went to church; he drank no wine; he never knew of the use of tobacco; and

1. In 1938 Harvard University appointed Walter Gropius Chairman of the Department of Architecture and Sigfried Giedion as Eliot Norton Poetry Lecturer. In 1963 Gropius et al designed the Pan-Am building over Grand Central Station and the old Penn Station was demolished, two facts which made it evident that something had gone terribly wrong in the culture of architecture over the previous quarter of a century. With pardonable exaggeration, I use hindsight to label both events, which curiously altered both of New York City's railroad stations, to mark the end of the 'modernism D.O.C.' in the USA.

although a naturalist he used neither trap nor gun [...] he had no temptations to fight against—no appetites, no passions, no taste for elegant trifles." Walter Gropius, a man of the twentieth century, showed quite an appetite for all of the above, but none whatsoever for history. *Thou Shalt Not Know History* was his motto.

Gropius' distaste for history was so strong and so radical that he alone among the so-called Masters of modernism, this isolationist man with ecumenical edges, was, as far as formal terms were concerned, ultimately rendered speechless by it. As far as speeches go, however, things were quite different. Gropius, as we know, was a German educator of international acclaim and this very fact won him the Harvard appointment. From the minute he set foot in Cambridge as head of the Department of Architecture, he spent his life in a fashion oddly similar to Emerson's. He wrote educational programs and sponsored exhibitions of his European doings, which reinforced his fame. Contrary to Emerson, however, he replaced the lectern with the pulpit and set himself the task of pursuing what he had failed to achieve as head of the German Bauhaus—an institute entirely devoted to the marriage of arts and crafts that, in spite of its name, never managed to formally house a department of architecture due, apparently, to a lack of funds. In Cambridge Gropius created a department of architecture or, in his terms, the "world's premier school for modern architects." This was the main goal of his life, namely, the ambition of "freeing the separate arts from their isolation and joining them together under the wings of architecture." Determined to dedicate his life to realizing "this concept," this is what by all standards he truly accomplished at Harvard, reducing architectural education to mere instrumental training. What this meant was the establishment of a *communauté des clercs*, made up of ardent believers and many novices, the latter of which were the most unconsciously gullible. With every trace of history out of sight (the antique details adorning Robinson Hall were actually taken out of the building), these 'modern' architects failed to develop any appetite whatsoever for history or historical precedents, while nurturing quite an insatiable one for reconfiguring the world through architecture. Like the first Christians, like the Pilgrims—all of whom professed the doctrine of predestination—the first modernists grew accustomed to believing that God or, rather, the spirit of the time, had predestined them to glory rather than to hell. It was inevitable therefore that, being avid readers of the New Bible—Giedion's book, that is—they thought of themselves as the chosen people. Guided by a messianic purpose, they firmly believed that they had been put on earth to remake cities. Giedion nominated them the third generation.

This cultural/theological juxtaposition grows more vivid when one looks at what happened to North American cities in the second half of the twentieth century. And this parallelism may help to address a question my notes left lingering: What impact did Gropius really have on his closest devotees? And to what extent did he mislead the group of people involved? This is the topic I would like to address—something that, to this day, I think, is still far from being widely understood.[2*]

2. *One should note that Gropius' chairmanship was characterized by a series of conflicts and can be subdivided into two different phases. In 1946 Marcel Breuer left the Faculty, broke his partnership with Gropius (arguably as a result of antagonism), and moved to New York to start a new practice. This marked the beginning of an open and personal war between Hudnut and

Let me continue by quoting Doctorow: "Thoreau's *Walden*, like Melville's *Moby Dick*, is a book that could only have been written by an American. You can't imagine this odd, visionary, but very thorough work coming out of Europe. It is peculiarly of us; it is indelibly made from our woods and water and New World ethos." This quote takes the scope of my investigation into a larger realm: the problem of the American author/architect and tradition. My previous notes register two things. First, that the modern American architect was supposed to come out of the precepts designed by Walter Gropius, the man who was widely expected to change the culture of architecture in a way that was perceived to be of timeless importance. Second, that Gropius was the man who decreed that all (architectural) books prior to 1938 should be forgotten.[3*]

Gropius, the main dispute of which was the infamous Basic Design course, which the former abhorred and the latter worshipped. By 1946, Hudnut understood that his idea of modernism differed radically from that of Gropius and that, inevitably, a battle for controlling the school and, by extension, the direction of Modern architecture, had to ensue. In hindsight, it is possible to identify 1946 as a turning point of the so-called Gropius Era at Harvard, one in which enthusiasm gradually gave way to disappointment and increasing anxiety in the school's various bodies. This was the year in which the only required history course was made an elective. What remains, however, is Gropius' final success in homogenizing all differences so that it is indeed possible to refer to a Gropius Era at Harvard.

3. [*]One should note that, at least at the beginning, Hudnut, who would eventually fight with Gropius over the most appropriate treatment of history, fully supported this move. As early as 1937 (before Gropius' arrival), he had already had history books—which he called deadwood—banished from Robinson Hall on the grounds that "History not only inhibited the making of a modern expression, but it stifled individual creativity."

The fact that of all institutions this happened at Harvard University, whose library system housed the widest book collection of the entire academic world, seems to be another irony of history. And the fact that the German National Socialists decreed the literal burning of all books patronized by Gropius at the same time as Gropius did appears to be another. This may help understand the mood (and the spirit) of the time and some of Gropius' possible motives. Yet, the fact that Gropius' two major operations—the systematic abolishment of tradition and the systematic abolishment of the idea of architecture as an art to the benefit of the idea of architecture as a somehow 'moral' science—should originate in one person and that this one person was celebrated as the shaper of Modern American architecture has been the source of endless anxiety and incredulity for me. Why did Gropius have such great appeal to American audiences? How is it possible that the zeitgeist doctrine resonated to the degree that it did, over an entire subcontinent for over a quarter of a century with no perceivable lessening of excitement in sight? Could there be a deterministic pattern behind this? Something that can explain why an institution like Harvard would appoint Gropius, the Master of European modernism, as the even more acclaimed Master of American modernism? This appears to be a contradiction in terms, given the intolerance that, as Doctorow seems to imply, the American grain appears to have—or is supposed to have—for organizations devoted to the arts? It is here that one suspects that Gropius' radical moves were enthusiastically accepted simply because they were a manifestation of another truly American phenomenon: the annihilation of the past for the benefit of the present. It is the relationship with the past, therefore, that must be brought into focus. What to make of it was, and still is, what is at stake—for Americans, at any rate. Isaiah Berlin once wrote that: “Only barbarians are not interested in where they came from, how they came to be what they are, where they appear to be going, whether they wish to go there, and if so, why, and if not, why not.” It is as if to say that the past is the past, and we cannot get rid of it. This is not what Gropius resolved to do, his interest lay in destroying the past.

My notes report that the fantasy of abolishing the past had already been formulated well before Gropius. Nathaniel Hawthorne did it in a parable called *Earth's Holocaust* and, a century earlier, Hawthorne's Puritan English ancestor, Oliver Cromwell, had seriously proposed burning the archives of the Tower of London so as to erase every memory of the past and start afresh, which, paradoxically, is one proof that the past cannot be eliminated. Sooner or later, ideas have their *ricorso,* as Vico would say—and among them, the project of eliminating the past. But the assumption underlying this issue—the nationalistic definition of the relationship between the American author and tradition—fills one with a skepticism that relates neither to the problem of Gropius' ambitions (which generated pathetic speculation instead of constructive theoretical reasoning) nor to the difficulty of the answer but to the very existence of the question. A pseudo problem? Some famous statements and interpretations made about the United States may prove helpful in articulating this. There is an opposition between Europe and America, an opposition between two areas of the globe, between two different attitudes about life and architecture. On the one hand, there are those who maintain that America is something new that American authors should celebrate; on the other, there are those who firmly believe that America is a mere continuation of Europe. J. M. Brown supported the former, Edgar Allan Poe the latter. Brown went so far as to write something that Melville would have liked, stating that he and his followers actually incarnated the former. This is not the only opposition in place, just the oldest. Perhaps it is not discussed as much now as it used to be, yet the history of American culture—and the history of American architecture (on the East coast in particular)—still reflects in one way or another the incessant conflict between these two conceptions. There are supporters on both sides. Doctorow: "*Walden* is one of the handful of works that make us who we are. *Walden* is crucial to the identity of Americans who have never read it and have barely heard of Thoreau." A bit further down the page he reports that Thoreau left a note saying that "near the end of March, 1845, I borrowed an ax and went down to the woods by Walden Pond nearest to where I intended to build my house, and began to cut down some tall arrow white pines...." This helped Doctorow to make the point that Americans are the independent entrepreneurs of themselves. He was sure of this and it remained, for him, a national heritage. Ralph Waldo Emerson, I think, would have agreed, as he was convinced that Americans, to be Americans, should have turned their backs to Europe and gone about their own business in their own way. The list goes on: In *Democracy in America* (1835) Alexis de Toqueville opined that the culture of a democratic people would never show much concern for the historical. In America, he wrote, "no one cares for what occurred before his time. In America each generation is a new people. Americans have no interest in keeping records. Democratic art and literature will not examine human beings in historical settings." To this he added: "Among a democratic people, poetry will not be fed with legends or the memorials of old traditions." Walt Whitman hoped that America would give rise to a class of native authors "fit to cope with our occasions, lands, permeating the whole mass of American mentality." In a public address entitled "Nationalism in Literature and Art" delivered in 1916 at the American Academy of Arts and Letters, President Theodore Roosevelt stated: "Of course, an over-self-conscious straining after a nationalistic form of expression may defeat itself. But this is merely because self-consciousness is almost a drawback. The self-conscious striving after originality also tends to defeat itself. Yet the fact remains that the greatest work must bear the stamp of originality. In exactly the same way the greatest work must bear the stamp of nationalism. American work must come out of our own soil, mental and moral, no less than physical, or it will have little permanent value."

The opposition is equally strong. As early as 1856 Eliot Norton maintained: "No nation on the American continent, which stretched from the Atlantic to the Pacific, could ever be intellectually great, but only physically comfortable. For science and art, we must look to countries penetrated by gulfs, bays and rivers, and interrupted by mountains, so that we could communicate easily with one another, as in Europe." D. H. Lawrence believed that "plumbing + saving the world were the two great American specialties." He was further convinced that "the American was a European when he first went over the Atlantic," that "he is in the main a recreant European still," and that "the Spiritual home of America was, and still is, Europe. This is the galling bondage, in spite of several billions of heaped-up gold. Your heaps of gold are only so many muck-heaps, America, and will remain so till you become a reality yourselves." For Henry James there was: "No state, a vague federal name, no kings, no churches, no armies, no diplomats, no countryside gentlemen, no palaces, no castles, no parochialism, no ruins covered by ivy, no cathedrals, no important universities, no politicians, no clubs: no Epson, no Ascot!," everything more or less that he sought in England, at least for his art. But James' statement is not as straightforward as it seems given that he is speaking about artistic creation and merely expressing his own resentment as an artist rather than making the case for history. On the contrary, he used the past to the extent that it was "amenable to imaginative penetration of social existence." What counts, rather than the subject itself, is what one can find in it, what one, as James of course did, makes of it. In other terms, the past is a fine place to visit so as to live more passionately in the present.

The list ends here with a contradiction worth remarking. It has been said that American authors should adhere to an Anglo-European tradition. This is what Lawrence supported. But a second more patriotic opinion sustains that, to be Americans, Americans had—and still have—to cut themselves off from the past and, in consequence, there can be no continuity between Europe and America. The second opinion matters because it rests upon the conviction that, for millions of people, the process of becoming an American has always meant a gradual process of self-imposed de-Europeanization. If this second patriotic thesis is true, how can one possibly explain Gropius? How can one explain the Harvard appointment? How is it possible that the greatest monument ever built to the Enlightment, the country that most exploited Locke's pragmatism and allergy to dogmatism, could have appointed the most dogmatic of all educators to the most powerful chair of the land? This appears to be a contradiction that, according to the Popper *principia*, would make the entire edifice collapse. Or should one assume that Gropius' acknowledgement of Locke's discovery that knowledge comes from experience was enough to justify his appointment? This accords with one thing: having seized upon the revolutionary aspect of the new mood of construction, Gropius may have ignited the greatest American aspiration of all, namely the rigorous abolition of historical precedent to the benefit of individual talent. But, as is well known, Gropius aspired to celebrate collaboration over self-worship, arguably as a result of his own physical disability.[4*] How, then, can those who assume forgetfulness, indifference to history, and the freedom from any authority outside the self to be the defining traits of American thought explain the Harvard appointment? That history has often found arid ground in the American landscape is, of course, no mystery. Yet the consequence of this would be to act, in Emerson's footsteps, in an individual, subjective, self-reliant, and master-less fashion. What is singular about modernism, however, beyond the extent to which it was implemented, is the fact that the push toward collaboration came from European 'Masters' who, once on the west side of the Atlantic, found themselves in an usual position. After having spent more than half a lifetime railing against power systems, they were invested with an unprecedented power that seems to have changed their nature—to say nothing of their psyche—cre-

---

4. *Due to cramps, Gropius hardly ever touched a pencil and made collaborative practice the hallmark of his career. His partners, in chronological order, were: Adolf Meyer and Carl Fieger in Germany, Maxwell Fry in England, Marcel Breuer and, last but not least, TAC—The Architects' Collaborative in America.

ating a condition that, in hindsight, may be responsible for having led them so far astray.[5*]

Let me confess my perplexity about the explanation sketched above. Let me also confess that it proved instrumental in helping me understand three things. First, the idea that all of these opinions were traditionally believed to be mutually exclusive and that one could only be accepted at the expense of the other: a condition that has made any author who asserted tradition feel as though they were working against the American grain. To me, it seems unfounded. One can understand that it may have been necessary in facing the problem of negative self-definition, or in justifying a declaration of solitude or of unprecedented loss. But everything that has taken place on one side of the Atlantic has had profound resonance on the other and this would hardly have occurred if one side were cut off from the other. Second, the idea that one should confine oneself to the national traits of one's own country in order to be considered a true artist of that country seems to be an intellectual fallacy of the greatest order. And perhaps it is necessary to say that this appears to be not only conceptually incoherent but also historically wrong. If this were not so, what should one think of Robert Adam, whose work was based on non-English precedents? I think Adam

---

5. At the Bauhaus, Gropius' declared goal was neither the pursuit of style nor dogma. At Harvard he appeared to have the opposite goal, one that was clearly based on style and dogma. The only part of his three-leg stool that did not change after his transatlantic move is his relentless search for a new aesthetic unity based on Marxist anti-aesthetic functionalism. Is this enough to avoid talking about Gropius' split personality? Walter Gropius the first—the Goethe-Gropius of Weimer—as opposed to Walter Gropius the second—the Harvard-Gropius of Cambridge?

would have been amazed if people had told him that, as an Englishman, he had no right to build his practice on examples found in Split. Third, the idea that all a priori discussion concerning the limits of artistic endeavors is based upon an even greater intellectual fallacy: that intentions and plans can be instrumental in creating a work of art.

This is why I unconsciously surrender to a voluntary dream that allows me to understand that, historically speaking, the vast measures I found so upsetting may be inextricably linked. My vision suggests that what Gropius set about to do may be why it was so successful, though it would be difficult to prove. All I can say is that, from my notes, the puritan set of values was based on the conviction that men needed some sort of external authority such as the Ten Commandments and the Bible as well as a set of highly educated spiritual leaders able to interpret the law (the Bible). Modernists shared similar convictions. The difference was that they replaced the Bible with Giedion's book, spiritual leaders with the Bauhaus faculty, and the pope with Walter Gropius. The shoes changed, as D. H. Lawrence would have said, yet the nature and the mode of consciousness remained the same: shared moral aspiration, shared value systems.

In 1924 D. H. Lawrence wrote: "Surely it is especially true of American art, that it is all essentially moral. Hawthorne, Poe, Longfellow, Emerson, Melville: it is the moral issue which engages them. They know nothing better, mentally!" This leads me to think that it would have been difficult to find more fertile ground for modernistic endeavors than the holy and puritan land of the newly relocated Englanders. Both were against ostentatious forms and rituals, elaborate ornaments, stained glass windows, and idolatrous statuary—in short both were anti-aesthetics to the extreme. More importantly, they both preferred worldly asceticism. Devotees of determinism might say that this is a confirmation of their doctrine and that it could not have been otherwise. More uncertain, I can only conclude that the historical luminosity of the place must have paved the way for the success of American modernism.

What, then, is the American tradition? Berkeley formulated a cyclical theory of history, maintaining that empires, like the sun, go from east to west—*Westward the course of empire takes its way*—and that the last and greatest empire of history would be that of America. Americans took note and decided to name one of their most western cities—Berkeley—after him. This restates some obvious facts. First, that America is the last significant manifestation of Western culture, a millennial culture made up of a plurality of authentic cultures that, though mutually intelligible, have their own points of view and their own value systems. Second, that American tradition, as Louis Kahn demonstrated, relies on themes coming from abroad. Third, that American architects can successfully belong to this noble American tradition in the same way as the treatment of Italian precedents belongs, thanks to Robert Adam, to English tradition.

I said that the problem of the American author/architect and tradition was a pseudo problem. I hope to have explained what I meant. I do not wish to interpret the conjectures contained in it but to stress, in conclusion, that I embrace, somehow simultaneously, both theses of the above opposition, in spite of their seeming incompatibility and that, paradoxically, I remain convinced of their mutual validity. I agree, in other words, that American art is both new and old. I agree that something unprecedented was founded with the creation of the United States, but that Anglo-

European tradition was a large part of it; that the latter was somehow reoriented, at times, in improvisational ways, for noble purposes, but that, at the same time, it was subject to mistake. In short, I think that architectural problems are filled with ethical questions, but that does not mean that architecture is a historical moral science, as Gropius believed. In other words, I acknowledge that American art, architectural departments included, is as artificial and imperfect as any other.

Post scriptum

The fact that I maintain all such judgments to be true and untrue, somehow simultaneously, is what, thanks to our conversations, I learned the most from Henry N. Cobb.

American Modernism 2.0: the global hoax

Berlin, 2020. Unpublished

Shifting the emphasis to aesthetics as a dimension experienced as satisfying in and of itself, devoid of the anxiety generated by its instant communication, or by the ambition to become notorious, or indifferent to the moment of its own publicity. To defend this possibility of life, which is so unlikely in our day—and defend it even in regard to works of architecture, whose experience is widely abused by schizophrenic fruition or pseudo-artistic ambitions, when not (on the 'cultured' side) by the prevalence of induced obligations of abstract erudition or misunderstood scientific seriousness, and violent knowledge—defending all this is not so obvious nowadays, nor is it meaningless. This piece attempts to do so by gathering notes on the cultural and professional consequences of the return of a misdirected American modernism which is sold as digitally inevitable.

We used to fight for what was right. We were fighting for moral reasons.
We passed laws, we annul laws, for moral reasons.
We declared war on poverty, not on the poor.
We made sacrifices. We cared about our neighbors.
We supported with money what we said we believed in. We never beat each other's chests.
We built great things, made incredible technological advances, explored the universe.
We cured diseases and built the world's largest economy. We have reached the stars.
We have acted like men. We believed in intelligence.
We didn't belittle it, because it didn't make us feel inferior.

Michael Sorkins, *The Newsroom*, 2015

Modernism was an aesthetic project that took center stage in history last century under a disguising light. Modernism, in fact, was introduced as being the single frame of mind necessary to impersonate modernity's best invention—the scientific method—which would cure the various sicknesses derived from rampant urbanization. Therefore, it is not surprising that modernism has often been confused with modernity, which is actually a project spanning 500 years. Its goal is to distinguish the real from the imaginary thanks to perpetual skepticism and verification based on empirical evidence. The main problem of Modernism turned out to be its main assumption: the ambition of being able to address the future assuming that all societies throughout the world would (and should) become one universal (identical) society, with one single (universal) space, one method of communication and one style available for one universal, modern (capitalistic-like) man. In other words, modernism was (and still is) a radical ideological project that is profoundly at odds with the complex diversity of the human fabric and, by extension, of architectural form, both of which stubbornly persist in opposing ways as neither radical nor ideological.

The main problem of modernism's primary ambition was that it invested the world of architecture with the *wrong* tone, or rather a tone that opposes the one (read: modernization) called for on that occasion. It was an inappropriate Protestant tone. Much like Luther's protest, it showed no signs of flexibility and left no room for argumentation. It was a tone that did not allow for counter voices or debate. It was a take-it-or-leave-it, intransigent and uncompromising tone of those convinced that they were on the right side of history. It was a take-no-prisoners tone: either you are with us or against us. If you are not with us, we have to take you down. The tone left no room for anything relevant or decisive for practicing architecture—chiaroscuro, internal debate or semantic ambiguity, or as expressed in a very apt German word that captures all of the above, a *Stimmung*—that was, on the contrary, washed away for the benefit of the self-proclaimed 'scientific' tone.

Today, a hundred years later, the tone has lost none of its rhetorical energy and it is fully blowing the sails of would-be new digital architects and urban planners with the important difference that this time, in the era of Modernism 2.0, the blowing has the full backing of the most formidable money-making machine the world has ever seen: turbo-capitalism. Currently, in other words, the advocates of the new digital solutionism are falling in the same trap the modernist did a hundred years ago: they keep delivering the very same false promises with the very same intransigent, uncompromising tone. They introduce themselves as the entity that is smart enough to cure sick old cities and turn them into 'smart objects.' They are specifically focused on aspects being more efficient, more functional and comfortable enough that urbanization itself may be experience by its users (users, not citizens) as if it were a politically-correct backdrop designed for a Netflix TV-soap-opera to be watched from a comfortable couch delivered by a drone. Few seem able to find the equation between cities and cars (or phones) preposterous enough, from an intellectual standpoint, to be compelled to publicly identify the new digital solutionism as a new version of the 'good old' modernist hoax. They also cannot admit that a number of risks associated with living in a city can never be eliminated, except at the cost of denying the essence of city living itself. As Reiner de Graf convincingly put it, 'the rhetoric of the smart city, for all the elevated language of its manifestos—and there are many—is driven by the pursuit of business interests, something that stands in stark contrast with the grand urban visions of the twentieth century, which celebrated the city as a public phenomenon.'[1]

---

1. Cfr. Reiner de Graf, *Four Walls and a Roof. The complex nature of a simple profession*, (Cambridge: Harvard University Press, 2017).

The New Man

Modernism had one big obsession of the genetic kind: the design of the New (modern) Man (as defined in the 1920s by Bauhaus). The New Man had to be psychologically and professionally whole. He was supposed to be forged through the process of purging, or un-learning, by surgically removing all assumptions previously held before he could enter the school itself, as Johannes Itten put it while he was in charge of the Preparatory Course (1919-1923). The idea was to rid the body of the human element through enemas, prolonged fasting, following a garlic-based diet and using machines to prick the skin in order to induce a trance-like delirium that would give access to a spiritual domain. When Moholy-Nagy, took over the responsibility of the course (1923), he set out to design the New Man as a whole unit, professionally and psychologically: a combination of multi-skilled whole-ism with staggering similarities to the new digital solutionists operating today in California. Moholy-Nagy tried to introduced a new way of seeing the world from all sides. It is curious to see how this trap worked for two relatively backward countries, culturally speaking: Prussia in the 1920s, and USA in the 1930s. At the time, USA was still in its imitation phase where it had to copy French or Italian models to 'catch up' with the 'wheels' of time. It is a well-known fact that it was not possible in USA to resist the opportunity to put to good work the recently available Bauhaus architectural migrants (in Boston and Chicago). That meant putting them in charge of designing the New Democratic (American) Man by giving people, just as Moholy-Nagy theorized, the opportunity to see things that were all around them and integrate those elements into their own unique individual experience. In the American context, they just had to drop the political, anti-capitalist attitude and substitute it with a capitalistic one. This would happen after they had been purged of any sense of historical precedents, which was not American in the first place, thus fulfilling the most American of all American ambitions.

Fast-forward a couple of decades to Black Mountain College in the 1950s, an art school in rural North Carolina that instantly turned into the 'new frontier' by its attempt to design the American version of the New Man: the artist-scientist designed according to the Bauhaus standard. It was a project that appears now to be based on *Happenings* (an item that would become a key feature of American life and art for almost a century) of a various kind: like studying music with John Cage, dance with Mark Cunningham, and painting with William de Kooning under the supervision of Bauhaus migrant Josef Albers. The most important New Man on campus from the architecture field was Bucky Fuller, of course. While there, he patented (not invented, as is typically believed) the object that would make him famous around the world—the geodesic dome—which appeared for a time and was discussed as being *the* solution to all of mankind's problems, new as well as old.[2] The techno-centered communal felt the renewed urge to implement the Bauhaus ambition by reaffirming design as the key tool. It was design purged of its overt political agenda, but not

---

2. So was his concept of comprehensive design, namely the process of taking badly distributed resources from the industrial world and putting them to work in a more holistic and organic fashion. The very tool of comprehensive design to be worked by the American invented scientist-artist was thought to be able to save the day, and the world.

of its hidden (Protestant) moral code, which is obsessively at the core of today's Silicon Valley. Currently in Northern California, the big problem is that the main business of its main player, the so-called GAFA (Google, Apple, Facebook and Amazon) has recently become a surveillance business conglomerate masked by providing the illusion that it allows people 'to connect' with the people they 'love.' When in fact, social media design today, quite literally being a new modality of social interaction, manages to sell people (and most of GAFA's employees) on the notion that a new human experience is now attainable (and arguably has already been attained): the dream of the workplace as a community of new (smart) men working to build a better world when, in fact, they are just monitoring the population of the entire world for the (financial) benefit of their bosses.

La Société du Spectacle

It could be considered pertinent to review a quick capsule history of the recent radical cultural change that the USA has half-unconsciously imposed on itself and, by extension, on the rest of the world. Up until sometime in the 1990s, the consensus centered around the idea that being allowed to live in the USA was the coolest thing one could do with one's life. Much like its presidency, the country was still very much perceived as serving as the 'leader' of the free and the *heimat* of free enterprise. This was particularly true for its educational establishments, in spite of the fact, as its graduates know, that the most interesting students able to enrich the educational environment were actually 'educated' outside of the USA.

A quarter of a century later, the number of American citizens who find it intolerable to live in the USA, or to stomach the news cycle that keep feeding itself on a daily basis at a speed that no one is equipped to follow, has reached a height that was simply unforeseeable one generation ago. The notion that pursuing an academic education in the USA may be a good idea holds true now only for some spoiled Chinese citizens who seem to think that an American 'degree' is the best marketable tool for self-promotional purposes.[3] What has become clear in a matter of less than a quarter century is that the value of self-marketing has become the only accepted 'value' brought about by a digital revolution which was officially unleashed to make the world a better (permanently connected) place. No one is surprised to see Ivy league establishments, specifically the establishments originally designed to help create an individual's critical consciousness, accepting it as the only worthy value and accepting them with no hesitation. American society has truly become the relentless engine of a social spectacle. This is thanks to a network of social media which is constantly mocking any traditionally accepted sense of privacy or social distance. It has taken control the world over by implementing what can be found word-by-word in the *libretto* that was produced with uncanny foresight by Guy Debord half a century earlier in a famous

3. It is interesting to note that no one ever remarks on this, as far as I know. At the height of their empire, the cives of Rome enjoyed the benefit of being at the center of the empire and they were entertained by a great deal of circensem, (150 days a year, to be precise). In contrast in USA, everyone is so enslaved by digital devices that they are unable to find 15 minutes of non-working status. One is left to doubt the benefits of having an empire to manage.

book. As predicted in Debord's *Societe du spectale* (1967), we all find ourselves, either willingly or unwillingly, immersed in a totally pervasive, generalized spectacularization as the one that singularly defines and unifies the elements of our lives. Spectacularization has become the ripe fruit of a financial capitalism that is spinning out of control. It is building its own epic of merchandise and passions.

La Société du Spectacle, unexpectedly described in detail by Guy Debord with the foresight of coming fifty years earlier, is now in place at the expense of everything else. To a large extent, *La Société du Spectacle* revolves around the ambition of stupefying the entire world. In the English language, the ability to stupefy is the ability to make someone unable to think clearly, usually because they are made extremely tired or have taken (stupefying) drugs. The verb—to stupefy—also means the ability to surprise or shock someone very much, making them 'stupid.'[4]

As far as value systems go, it is remarkable to note the complete U-turn performed by American society on itself within the timeframe of a generation. Gone are the

---

4. As far as architecture is concerned, this stupid-making process has emerged as of late with stunning clarity thanks to the relentless work of an easily identifiable iconoclastic gang (Libenskid, Morphosis, Diller/Scofidio and the like), i.e. the people who think that architectural form is a vehicle for mass-communication whose main purpose is communication itself. Notoriously operating out of the very center of *La Société du Spectacle,* (the USA, that is) the gang has managed to produce and market the necessity of covering the earth's crust with 'spectacular' projects. The work of this gang might be best summed up in its aspiration by one of its exegete, Aaron Betsky: 'to think of a way where gravity disappears, perspective bends or deforms, lines converge and the definition of scale or activity is lost.' They are a bunch of would-be *maitre-a-penser* who 'theorize' that, in order to be an 'important' architect, it is important to do the opposite of what Wittgenstein recommended: be strong enough to resist most temptations.

traditional values—see epigraph—that once stood at the core of American life, defining it as a new 'experience' on the world stage. Beyond the ambition to save the world (that would rather prefer to be left un-saved and not become the unwillingly beneficiary of 'exported democracy'), what is not gone is what should be gone: the deeply moralistic Protestant stance of the 'new modernists,' who find themselves this time around being busy with an a-critical, sometimes merciless, sponsoring behaviour of the new 'digital, algorithmic values' that no one appears to be able to criticize, much less resist. It is an attitude that typically knows no uncertainty or self-doubt, in spite of the fact that the turbo capitalism that is in the process of being reached at an ever increasing speed. Even the world of finance seems unable to tame this type of capitalism. The end goal was brilliantly described almost a century ago by Walter Benjamin himself: self annihilation.[5]

The new American way can now be defined as turbo capitalism, incarnating the most extreme and absolute cult that ever existed: a cult that knows no 'off-days' but rather one long uninterruptable working day that keeps marching on like perennial clockwork. It is a clock which is 'sustained' by unending lines of 'credit' that, differently from the religion that it has replaced (or secularized, depending on who is doing the speaking), has substituted redemption, or atonement of guilt, with guilt itself. Hope is gone. Technology rules. There is no opposition to speak of. For the

5. Cfr. Walter Benjamin, *Capitalismo come religione*, (Genova: Il Melangolo, 2013); Giorgio Agamben, *Mezzi senza fine. Note sulla politica*, (Torino: Bollati Boringhieri, 2016); Giorgio Agamben, *Creazione e anarchia. L'opera nell'età della religione capitalistica*, (Vicenza: Neri Pozza editore, 2017).

vast majority of its former believers, the American dream has now turned into a (bad) Freudian nightmare that is best described by Freud's own turn of phrase: the 'capital on which the hell of the unconscious pays its dividends.'

A society based on the cult of credit, a society that has made credit its only belief, is condemned to live in perennial debt. Yet, contrary to the XX century's accepted common sense rules (most notably the 1933 Glass-Steagall Act) that the Clinton administration deemed pre-digital and therefore outdated, there is no correspondence left between the financial sustainability of the activity being performed and the extent of the lines of credit granted for performing it.[6] The lines of credit are, in fact, unstoppable not only for the one generation that requests them, but for all the generations to follow, for the rest of time. Hence the need to put to good work (for financial gains) Guy Debord's central thesis: the incessant production of images and forms to be amassed as heaps which are spectacular enough to distract the audience from the real issue that needs to stay hidden: the issue of the entire world population turning into one digital, narcissistic junkie that is unable to stop uploading personal information and therefore unable to spend more than a few minutes away from the terminal

6. Many analysts consider (with reason) the repeal of the 1933 Glass-Steagall Act by the Clinton administration the single act that opened the door to the unsustainable world that followed, the world in which turbo capitalism was left free to turn the entire world into a permanent casino in which the chips seem to be permanently down and all bets are off, for almost everyone except a dozen predatory tech companies that are increasingly busy communicating their philanthropic endeavors to distract people from perceiving the fact that they keep prospering in a cycle that is out of control thanks to some legalese paperwork that make it 'legal' for them to avoid paying taxes the world over.

that dictates the agenda of every single human being: the smart phone or tablet. The spectacle of real or presumed money has become the only spectacle allowed. This is because the totality of the use has been interchanged with the totality of abstract representation.[7]

Modernism 2.0

It is no surprise if architectural form, within the current cultural scenario, has been turned into a commodity whose commercial 'value' is a function of its own digital iconic power, specifically the ability to generate an algorithmic interest that comes with one big marketing advantage: the fact that it can be 'measured' on social media. The more instant likes it gets on Instagram, the higher its value. For over a quarter of a century now, this has caused a number of American designed global viruses that, much like the current coronavirus. They have spread very quickly across the world—blob architecture, hyper-modernism, over-design, parametricism, etcetera. They have all done their best to make people forget the nature of building itself, as if architectural form could be considered nothing more than a fancy dress to be used for one single social event or party.

In the last quarter century, architecture has increasingly been reduced to a number of *slogans* that can be effortlessly copied and pasted by journalists into new and old media

7. Cfr. The Social Dilemma, a 2020 American docu-drama documenting the rise of social media and the damage it has caused focusing on the exploitation and manipulation of its 'users' for financial gain through data mining and surveillance capitalism.

headlines or slogans, as if it were a piece of ghostwriting for a condensed political speech to be delivered on Zoom to an audience that is perennially distracted by a constant feed of Google alerts about urban meltdown. Populism has become the weapon of choice: only the most obvious and easily digestible propositions and proposals will survive in this kind of an environment. A new seemingly comic-book directedness has set in as a sort of caricature of the design process itself. It is a LEGO-like architecture that is immediately available to be inserted in a relentless circulation of images managed through the hottest digital platform of the day. It is accessible for a public increasingly accustomed to the most daring visual promiscuity of social-media driven architecture and late-capitalist spectacular shock. It is a dead-pan formal concept. This concept is manipulated to generate a process which, in turn, can generate a new form that is capable of expressing something old modernity itself lacked the strength to achieve.[8]

What characterizes the present trend is the belief of that there are no limits to worry about: to go beyond the modern, the process needs to travel totally freely, without fixed limits and breaking down any conventionality. The non-stop nature of social media working 24/7/365 erases the relevance of the subjects per se in reality. The emergence of new image-based media feeds an absent debate in which news about buildings becomes available instantaneously and immediately while being reduced to a myriad of casual and low-resolution pictures, which are consumed as they get built.

---

8. A good summary of the current situation was delivered by Alejandro Zaera-Polo called *Well into the XXI century. The Architectures of Post-capitalism?* on El Croquis, 187, 2016

'The spectacle is the money' writes Debord, 'that can only be looked at, since in it the tonality of the use is exchanged with the tonality of the abstract representation.' As is self-evident, the spectacular use of architectural form turns that architectural form itself into a physical manifestation of the power of money in the public eye, even though the message being communicated seems to be communication itself, as there is nothing else that needs to be 'communicated.' In other words, unbridgeable gaps have set in between the perception of architectural form and its ontological nature. These gaps also concern the unnatural detachment of architectural form from the figurative world of its own tradition. Free from the constraints of conventionality, as a process, architecture has become mere research of easily expendable forms, and it is increasingly careless about the relationships that such form should entertain: it is careless about the context, careless about the resources, and careless even about its own livability. Inattentive because unlimited is the architecture of the American modernism 2.0. In a glowing expressive emphasis, it has not stopped at designing the architectural object, but has expanded to 'design' every kind of object imaginable.

The spectacle of kitsch

What has become increasingly clear today is that this new American modernism of pure process, more than of new horizons, has opened the way to a new form of spectacle that few foresaw: the spectacle of kitsch.[9] The definition of

9. The topic was put on the table by valerio mosco. Cfr: http://www.

kitsch varies from author to author, much like its etymological origin, but many still agree that kitsch is ultimately an attraction for ostentatious excess in which the effect prevails over the cause.[10] In other words, it is a form of cheap romanticism like a soap opera, for example, that monumentalizes the superficial to hide the lack of principles. To put it another way, the new modern digital Kitsch mystifies as new what is exactly the opposite of new. It boasts a spirituality that is simply missing or absent. Much like traditional kitsch, it is the result of three conditions. Firstly, it presents an object deemed as beautiful within an emotive sphere. Secondly, it is immediately recognizable. Thirdly, it does not enrich the associations we can have with its subject in any substantial way. Taken together, these three conditions make the parasitic nature of kitsch evident and reveal its deceptive quality. Kitsch does not create its own beauty. This comes about because its appeal is not really generated by the aesthetic merit of the work itself, but by the attractiveness of the object represented, which often amounts to an aesthetic catastrophe.

At least as far as aspiration goes, an unbreakable link connects space and social behavior as the new kitsch also

---

zeroundicipiu.it/2016/04/10/larchitettura-kitsch-di-zaha-hadid/

10. Some believe that the term kitsch comes from the English word sketch, that appeared around 1870s in the field of art dealing, where it identified the pantomime that the merchants displayed to devalue the artworks available in the market. However, the majority of scholars think that it comes from the German word Kitschen, which has the meaning of 'collecting street junk as well as selling new things as if they were old.' It also identifies bad taste. This is nothing new, of course, but people who utilize it stylistically and consciously forfeit any intention of authenticity in order to opt for lies, imitations (quotation) or a taste for serial reproduction as their own horizons.

aims at directly influencing the behavior of its 'users.' The new kitsch actually presupposes 'kitsch users,' those who are like drug users (addicts) and crave being unequivocally married to bad taste, as well as ostentatious and gratuitous forms. The new modern kitsch is also expressed through technical precision and a profusion of means that is often much too exorbitant. It does not accept compromise with the unfinished, and with what is worn out over time, that in turn cannot do without at least a share of conventionality. To people living outside it, the vast majority of recent North American architectural production appears to summarize all these 'aspirations' in a paradigmatic way. It also demonstrates the fate of radical, or presumably radical unconventionality, which, once again, can only fall into the kitsch department.

The global hoax

As Howard Burns put it, traditionally architecture is the very art that mediates between conventionality and novelty, or between enthusiasm and understatement. Without convention, architecture evaporates into a vacuous game of effects that bores the eye as quickly as it astonishes. What American academia seems to have yet to understand, (perhaps because it is waiting to be told from the lips of some global guru belonging to a minority in need of protection) is that conventionality, being poetic, must be the object of a transference. It is to say that it should be reconfigured without overlooking one key aspect: at the end of the day, architecture is still is a matter of building, and it needs to talk about the condition of humanity, not about a miscellaneous intellectual bric-a-brac construed for the purpose of personal *réclame*.

The reflection on the importance of limits, the denial of form as a process, and the denial of per-formative form, together with the conviction that only by transfiguring the usual can one obtain poetic work, are what bind today's most convincing architectural practices together. The latter are able to perceive the global intellectual hoax produced by a century of modernism and see what it really is: a sort of con artist job fabricated by those who intend to sell the notion that architectural form can be a vehicle to save the world, where datafication can keep producing the trap set by Gropius a hundred years ago to date: the happy wedding of art, time and technology.

On the contrary, architecture remains an art of dissimulation, transfiguration and aesthetic transference that resists all forms of hyper-figuration or hyper-communication. Architectural form can only be an art that is difficult to obtain, a form or resistance that carries traces of its poetic relationship. This is not through the linear (read: chronological) sense of time introduced by the modern, but through notions of time that are indifferent to the digital compulsion of the day.[11]

From this point of view, a truly contemporary form of architecture is a place of inter-exchange of pathos between the many temporalities that shape the present time and its chaos, without any ambition to dominate. It just seeks to provide a figure of it.[12]

---

11. For a stark critique of the linearity of time introduced by the modern, the reader is referred to the remarks made in note 4 of the preliminary remarks that apply here as well.

12. Cfr. conrad-bercah, Berlin Transfert, An atlas of aesthetic ideas, (Siracusa: LetteraVentidue Edizioni, 2021).

APPENDIX

Immigrant architects?

New York City, 1997. Unpublished

This is the text of an oral presentation I delivered on April 29, 1997 at the Harvard University Child Memorial Library to meet the requirements of the Longfellow Fellowship bestowed by the English and American Literature Department. As suggested by its epigraph, it reads as a sort of overly enthusiastic delivery of a spirited argument expressed by someone holding an overly idealistic notion about the life an architect. It is presented here in the appendix to entertain the reader.

Asked about mass-media influence, Norman Mailer once remarked—in a line worthy of Norman Mailer—that the "more people you reach in any mass-media form, the less you will be able to say per unit. If you are talking to three people, you will affect history as much as if you talk to three million or thirty million people. By the time you are talking to thirty million people, you will say things like "we have got to balance the budget."

Before starting, let me tell you how aware I am of the difficulty of the job I am supposed to perform here today. It is almost a rule than the more complex a job is, the lesser its billing. And yet to deliver thoughts in front of a highly sophisticated audience—and this is arguably as sophisticated as it gets—is always difficult and seldom relaxing. Especially if one is attempting, as the present speaker is, to balance some sort of budget, whether or not culturally bounded!

Be that as it may, in order to balance the budget of architectural accounts, something which is extremely unbalanced, I have some things to make clear so as to avoid misunderstandings. I know they accuse me of arrogance, and perhaps of madness. And yet I have to tell you that I am not who you think I am. Even though my presentation is today advertised to be delivered by a fellow named Paolo Bercah, I should state at the outset that this is not entirely correct: my name is, in fact, Richard Neutra and I am using Paolo's voice (with mutual discomfort) to deliver a few thoughts.

I am an American architect and, above all, a lover of architecture and cities—American ones, particularly. A lot of people fail to understand how this is possible. Individuals usually ask silly questions. Such as: How can one ever fall in love with American cities? Such a question is ridiculous. Please do not get me wrong. I am well aware of the fact that many American cities are in a state of decay; but I am also aware that they represent a moving possibility, arguably the last "possibility" that our lost Western civilization has provided its citizens with. But I do not feel like saying anything more about this. If one fails to see this, it is useless for me to try to gather evidence. If one is ignorant of the happiness and *joie de vivre* that American cities incarnate for us, it is difficult for me to explain it.

There is another ridiculous falsehood standing between me and the audience. The falsehood is that I am willing to talk about immigrant architects! Shall I repeat that I am American (Austrian-born) and that I do not count myself among the fashionable makers of the heroic "architecture in exile"? It is true that I was born in Imperial Vienna in 1892, but does that mean that I will be forever labeled as a Viennese architect? Even my detractors admit that I never practiced architecture there and that, on the contrary, I left her in her own depressing postwar status to find a place to be comfortable in. Not an easy task. Switzerland did not make it for me. Neither did Berlin. Or, for that matter, Mendelsohn. How can one work for somebody who estimates himself nothing shorter than *the* creator, and who is said to have said: "If God did not need assistants in creating the universe, why would I need one?" That he actually said so, I can here myself testify to.

Yet, the fact is that I have to be thankful to him. He made clear to me how this country, and this country only, would have been, for me, a possible place to practice this beloved discipline of mine. At least so I thought the minute I reached California. Not so much Chicago, where I worked for Holabird and Roche, or Frank Lloyd Wright's Taliesin, where I stayed in 1924. Taliesin, in all frankness, welcomed me with open arms, but then Mendelsohn came to visit and I had to serve as an interpreter. This was meant to smooth out all the terrible things that he had to say about *Amerika* and its immense landscape. Not particularly interested in those kinds of activities, the train to California was, for me, just a natural thing to step into: all the more because Rudolph Schindler, another buddy of mine, had already been there since 1914, and since that day he had continuously stimulated me to join him there.

Of course, I knew that California would have been my country and Los Angeles my hometown, well before moving there. It was like coming home, really. A stroke of luck acquired me membership to the most advanced circle in all Europe: the one revolving around the persona of Adolf Loos, who, needless to say, is the Austrian architect who restlessly walked lots and lots of American downtowns a century ago, namely from 1893 to 1896, and grew its American experience so much into himself that, once returned to Vienna, he naturally had to spit it out to radically change not only Viennese but architecture *tout court*. I have never met any person, either in this or any other land, who was as enthusiastic about the "States" as Adolf Loos. Adolf Loos was, by all means, my first American father. He had a deep influence on me. I have said it in my book already: "Adolf Loos was the first European naturally gifted with creative talent to discover for himself the happy efficacy of the American life-style, which he used as a starting point for his career." The houses he did in Vienna at the turn of the century were so inspiring to me for their "pleasant matter-of-fact comfort, especially when compared with the contemporary *Sezessionstil*," that I just could not possibly postpone my trip any longer. But is this enough to talk about immigrant architects? I myself would be much more comfortable to talk about migration rather than immigration. I am aware that this is the title that has been put to my presentation, but this is not enough to prevent me to tell you that I see things in a different light. And I mean from telling you why this afternoon. Can I add to my excuse that I had nothing to do with it?

But let us not continue with these sickroom complaints. To tell you the truth, I am very pleased to be here because I finally have the opportunity to direct some attention to a book I published in 1930 called *Amerika* that, I am sorry to admit, is far less known than another one carrying the very same title and written by my former employer: Erich Mendelsohn. The fact is that Mendelsohn published his four years before mine, and his book became so popular that it was almost impossible for me to change the European perception of this country—an issue that is still far—I dare say very far—from being resolved.

Since I have been trained to be precise, I should here say that, to be exact, the books in question are not two but rather four, as we both published two books each. Mendelsohn published *Amerika, Bilderbuch eines Architekten* in 1926; and *Russland, Europa, Amerika: ein architektonisher Querschnitt* in 1929. I published *Wie baut Amerika*? in 1926 and *Amerika; Die Stilbindung des neuen Beuens in den Vereinigten Staaten*, in 1930. But what is their reputation? Now, I know that one might suppose that a broad agreement among historians of modern architecture exists about Erich Mendelsohn's *Amerika* (1926). And that, in many ways, the book is called a classic of modern architectural literature. Describing the role and the influence of the book in shaping a European vision of the American landscape, Reyner Banham is unambiguous: "*Amerika,* together with his subsequent book *Russland-Europa-Amerika* of 1928, became a prime source of Modern Movement imagery for the rest of the 20s and 30s." Jean Louis Cohen maintains that "*Amerika* was a dazzling success in the bookstores, and was reprinted several times in the year of its publication."

But why on earth did historians always fail to underline how my *Wie Baut Amerika?* was immediately accepted by the foremost houses in Europe and at once became what was called a best seller? Let me tell you this. In 1930 I took a year-long globe tour, and I discovered that the book had been received with interest in Tokyo, Rome, Paris and all around the globe, because it reflected actual day-to-day experience and dealt with the miraculous American production in which the world had become interested, and that organizational know-how in relation to architecture. As a matter of fact, soon after publication, promoters considered it worth while to use my title for a huge exhibition which was then opening in Berlin. Let me assure you: the book sold like hot cakes!

My *Amerika*, the book I really want to talk about today, was, in fact, just the natural consequence of that success. Joseph Gartner commissioned it from me for Schroll as a part of a series of three books gathered under the rubric New Building in the World (*Neues Bauen in der Welt).* For it I dug out what I could of pioneer's work. I photographed the work of Sullivan's office boy, Irving Gill, whose friend and admirer I became. I collected the work of my old friend Schindler, who had contributed and learned much—perhaps too much for his own good—in Mr. Wright's office. I began to give my story of John W. Root and his beautifully integrated Monadnock Block; of Louis Sullivan, who mastered rich ornaments of his own gifts and spun them over parts of a nobly conceived soaring skeleton, and also over the concepts of Wright, his first great assistant. After so many years I can say in all fairness that this text is hardly dated, and it still makes worthwhile reading.

Unfortunately, no English version are available to the English reader and rare German prints of it lie in some rare collections over this country. But this is not enough to prevent one from investigating it with a larger lens. Or, for that matter, to compare it with Mendelsohn's *Amerika*. Will you allow me to do so? Before being thrown off the podium, I assume that you will. I believe that Mendelsohn's *Amerika* is worth examining precisely because of its editorial fortune—one based on a rather personal and superficial understanding of the American cities. Can one describe Mendelsohn's intentions as primarily historiographic? Hardly! With this book, an album where pictures are accompanied by telegraphic and sometimes poetic comments, Mendelsohn wanted to make, in his own word, "the admiring eyes" of the European observer of the American reality "more conscientious." May I add that, to rely on Banham again, "it gives us a sense of what a European modernist of the time *wanted* to see, or go out of his way to see." To be sure, Mendelsohn wanted to sketch a vision of the New World and the medium he used to do so is, in retrospect, highly visionary indeed.

I'd dare to say that, intellectually, *Amerika* is the inevitable consequence of Mendelsohn's direct contact with leading personalities of Modernism. As a matter of fact, the album is a sort of journal of Mendelsohn's own touring of the Northeast part of the country—a tour made in the company of Holm and Fritz Lang. In many ways the book can be described as a testimony—a rather distorted one—about American landscapes based on personal experience. It represents a "regurgitation" of that experience which, not surprisingly, was just two months long. Let me remind you this: every traveler is accustomed to this condition: this mixture of fatigue and apprehension—I can confirm this, having been a great traveler myself. It happens all the time that one begins to explore a territory charted by others but not by the present traveler who, as a matter of fact, is ready to introject every experience in a rather peculiar way. Imagination and misrepresentation are probably high on the list of every traveler, and the Amerika that Mendelsohn formed in his mind during and after his visit with Fritz Lang as a companion was a fusion of highly dramatic black-and-white movies and the prophetic attitudes of the day: the twenties.

Some hold the impression that his book is but the printed version of a more powerful film: Fritz Lang's *Metropolis*. The film, it is true, was produced right after their American Tour, and, therefore, can be seen as the result of it. I do not pretend to establish here whether or not that was indeed the case, even if I consider this reading plausible. As far as I am concerned, I can say that I never felt fatally attracted to *prophetic* attitudes, as I was more interested in American energy and optimism and wanted to understand better what the U.S. had produced in order to add something on my own. My book was the first, I believe, to evaluate the classical large American office, the big architectural office which, when I came here, was greater than anything that existed or could even be imagined in the old country.

But this was not, by any means, all I was interested in. Will you allow me to make my point by quoting from my 1924 article in *Architectural Record*? "Truly creative architecture should not concern itself with space forms created by structural members since these are subject to dimensioning. Our creative sense is concerned instead with proportions and surface treatments of rooms." What did

Mendelsohn have to say about this? Not much, I'd argue. In fact, Mendelsohn's album does not seem to be much concerned about architecture per se, but rather with American lifestyle which, needless to say, he failed to understand. Let us take a quick look at it. The book revolves around a hidden evaluative and evolutionary structure. Mendelsohn himself gives us some hints in the closing paragraph of his introductory piece. There he says that "this country gives everything: the worst strata of Europe, abortions of civilization, but also hopes for a new world." The headings according to which the material is organized follow a similar structure: from the "Typically American Traits," through Enhanced Civilization, The Financial Center, The Gigantic, and the Grotesque to finally land onto the The New—The Coming, the only section where architectural questions come into the picture. Commenting on a shot of the Tribune building under construction, Mendelsohn writes that "the bare bones of the construction force the truth upon us. When it can still be seen without cladding, the skeleton shows, more clearly and splendidly than the finished building, the boldness of construction with iron or reinforced concrete. Of course, it remains merely a skeleton and still awaits an equivalent expressiveness of form."

May I reply to this, saying once again that it is industry that "determines architectural styles?" And that "Spanish, Italian or English ornaments do not give the character of style to American houses so much as do the technical equipment, the roller screen, the impressive surface finish of walls and fixtures, the plate glass and enamel, tile, washable paints, hardware, and so on and so forth: all these parts of a clean cut environment proclaim that the buildings are of the twentieth century." I hold that the symbolic expression of the static function is as sincere as naïve and, furthermore, that x-rays of the finished building does not interest me the littlest bit.

On the contrary I had always been more attracted to traffic questions, railroad patterns and, above all, the financial and technical bases upon which this country built itself. The traffic question are, of course, not touched upon in Mendelsohn's. Yet they were—they still are—very important, and a section of my *Amerika* is devoted to them, even though my Rush City Project is much discussed in my first book. Henry Russell Hitchcock wrote (1927) in *Architectural Record* that "with the architect of 'Rush City' as with the architect of Pessac, of Dessau, or of Rotterdam, architecture is the aesthetic crystallization of the engineering solution of the building problem. Creation is again, as in the time of the great structural architecture of the past, a possibility, and nowhere more so than in America."

This brings me to the super-personal style issue. I hold that "the inventiveness of the American building supply market exacts the most intimate influence on contemporary style formation. Compared with this deeply rooted influence of mass production and world-wide marketing of building materials, the activity of even the most gifted progressive architect might be considered as secondary in importance as a reflection only of the essential super personal events. National style characteristics naturally recede to the background." Furthermore, I hold that "the multiplicity, acceleration and frequency of architectural work makes large-scale coordination essential, together with a considerable restriction of personality of the designer; this is well known to have occurred in remote periods of history, although it was not due to the same causes."

I feel compelled to add to this and expend a few words on standard and standardization. "Mass production and credit, characteristic of North America in particular, with its continent-wide market which is rapidly crossing the country's frontiers, are based on standardization. In the US more so than elsewhere, standardization means not only accepting generally recognized shapes and sizes, but also establishing their market values and manufacturing processes and methods. One of the characteristics of mature standardization is the possibility, possibly of French origin but used to the full for the first time in the US, of making identical construction elements inter-changeable so that repair work becomes a simple task rather than requiring a craftsman's skill."

But what exactly was the significance of standardization back then? I would say this: "In the century of great technology, exact prior calculation and calculation of the sizes of all parts, together with their determination in the technical specifications, has become the basic characteristic of building design. Without generally accepted standards devised by the various disciplines making up the construction field, this exact prior determination would be unthinkable and impossible."

Mendelsohn never thought of that. Or at least never used his book to express his point of view. All in all, Mendelsohn's story of *Amerika* is a very peculiar one. The album looks more like a screenplay than anything else. It documents (in a powerful way, I have to admit) the tempestuous growth of the twentieth century. A restless sense of energy and multiple activities permeates all its shots. Mendelsohn, or rather Lonberg-Holm (the photographer) made American cities look like warehouses/factories where human activities are stacked one on top of the other. One can see people running on the sidewalks while clouds of steam erupt from the street; litanies of automobiles, train-cars, and trams swinging by; in short, a sequence of prints filmed at a very accelerated pace. My story is much, much different. In my *Amerika* I spoke of American industrialized architecture, and, following the enthusiasm of Tacitus for his exemplary *Germania*, slanted so much my description that all the world thought there was much here to be taken to heart and that, in 1926, there was an American vogue for modern architecture. This was, of course, a downright untruth, I must now admit: I was terribly lonely, and was just whistling in the dark. One need only look at the magazine illustrations of that bygone age!

But I have to say something about the twenties. And about America and her supposed un-modern frame of mind. As I said before, I was one of the earliest European artists who emigrated *voluntarily* to the US, whereas Mendelsohn, after a short visit in 1926, was forced to do so in 1941, after having spent almost a decade abroad, mainly in England and Palestine. This brings me toward my main point—one that is in contradiction with the credo of the land. It has to do with the phenomenon of "modernity": an hot potato by any standard. In the last century European culture has always looked to the United States as the country where it was possible to realize the dream of modernity. Or, to say the least, as if it were the country where the *technological apparatus* together with a well-established social tradition would allow one to think it in concrete and operative terms. Even though the initial "ideas" of the avant-garde constituted the formalized core of the "project of modernity" in contemporary arts, the American dream, or its myth, never failed to play an important role.

This is well known. Yet, this credo bothers me. What bothers me is how the traumatic political events of the thirties have polluted the picture to the extent that, sadly enough, a widely spread falsehood—otherwise called common knowledge—has it that the political tragedy of European fascism led to the Cultural Diaspora that brought to the U.S. many of the avant-garde; the "modernization" of the country being the result. This is what I would call "the classical interpretation." I know, of course, that this took place. We all know it. Yet this form of "imported" modernization was not the only one that took place. If many followed the avant-garde's leaders in a state of harmless admiration of their successes, one should nonetheless realize how modernization in architecture, as in any other arts, was a matter of much wider significance. It could not possibly have been a single-edged concept. Nor did it belong to a small number of individuals. It is indisputable that an autonomous "modernization" was already underway within the US in the first quarter of the century—well before the Cultural Diaspora occurred. Such modernization was more a matter of facts than of convictions.

My case is emblematic. And I am in good company, I think: a large number of individuals, mainly architects and business-men, came to visit or live in the US long before they were forced to do so. The point of view that I am attacking is related to the theory of the one-sidedness of "modernity" in architecture, as it derived from the notorious 1932 MoMA exhibition called *The International Style*. I am already aware that this will sound odd to many of you, and I already see eye browse rising. Easily accessible evidence reveals in fact that I was the only American "architect of the west" who made the 1932 MoMA short list, the one that even Mendelsohn, with great scandal, did not make, and that Alfred Barr used to refer to me, among American architects, "as second only to Frank Lloyd Wright" in my international reputation. Easily accessible evidence also reveals that a building of mine—the 1927 steel-framed Lovell house—had become “indispensable to the iconology of modern architecture.”

Of course I was flattered to be on such a list, and I did help a hell of a lot to make the exhibition touring the country and finally landed in Los Angeles at the time when the 1932 Olympic Games were under evolution. The good thing about this is that it brought a lot of attention to architecture, lots and lots of press coverage, and subsequent commissions, by the hundreds, for me and my collaborators. But you tell me what you would have done in a similar case!

Nonetheless, I cannot be confused with the cultural stance embedded in it, though my ego might so desire. The fact is that I disagree with this theory. I was never, and am still not, interested in superimposed artificial coherence. Nor in what one man—three men in this case—may want to link together. Many may have thought that in 1932 a new currency, the International Currency in terms of forms, demanded to be forged, in order to provide the market with a new, potent, buying power with which to “balance the budget”; but, as for Schindler and for me, America was “*un pays déjà classique du progrès, des solutions élastiques, sans cesse changeantes, rigoureusement adaptées aux exigences du business et du confort*”—as Julius Poelzig remarked in 1931 while reviewing my book on “L’Architecture d’aujoud’hui.”

It is, in consequence, inevitable for me not to spend a few “cents” to comment on this and provide my point of view. Like many other (philosophers), I think that at the turn of the century a rather interesting twist occurred along immigration highways, and “trips of studies” gradually supplanted "trips of hopes." There are many possible examples of this. But I do not want to go through such a tedious list. Everybody knows them. What I want to point out is that in many ways one can say that along the 20th century the most famous *Grand Tour* (upon which the architectural education has been relying for so many centuries) gave way to the rather less noble although more appropriate *American* (Enormous) *Tour*.

To make the question of America's immensity more clear to the audience, I would need to draw from Claude Lévi-Strauss's *Tristes Tropiques*, as I hold that his description has the authority of something proven by facts. But unfortunately we do not have the time to do so, and, therefore, I can only recommend that you go through it once again. What I can do is to advertise my case as a demonstration of that. By 1925 it had become clear to me that the United States was a wide, diversified land and that New York and Chicago were only important parts of it. To tell you the truth, I had a premonition of that well before 1925. Once when I was walking down the Bahnhofstrasse in Zurich, I saw in a travel-office window a folder with a palm tree printed on it, and the words, "CALIFORNIA CALLS YOU." I knew only a little English then, and I wasn't quite sure what this meant, but I put two and two together and concluded that I was supposed to come to California. After I had been in New York, Chicago, and Taliesin, I began restlessly to think about California. I made up my mind in the winter of 1925.

Frank Lloyd Wright and Walter Gropius, I understand, have not spoken too favourably about California. But it was to turn out the most contemporary southland in search of a way of life for this day. Mies and Le Corbusier never visited there, as far as I knew. If they had, they would hardly have felt friendly toward its cultural naïveté, bordering everywhere on "mix up." Me, Loos had educated, I guess, to sympathy with "lowly mix-up." For me Los Angeles was a very peculiar spot and vantage point. It was clear that this romantically Spanish colonial country of California might become a prototype for industrial and research area, emulated by many others who could only artificially develop the *climate control of tomorrow*.

Is it really necessary, at this point, to say that this condition of mine was but another case of a long-term tradition? And to say that such a tradition was founded by the first informed traveler, my beloved Adolf Loos, who, as I said before, left for the United States in 1893 not to visit the World Colombian Exposition, as has been said, but with the firm intention of becoming familiar with the American way of life? I was told many times by Loos himself how he could not bear to stay in Chicago more than four weeks and, instead, could ever get enough of New York, even if he did not work as an architect and, instead, spent all his time in restaurants, YMCA rooms, washing dishes, and, above all, in walking (equipped with his beloved American shoes) along the streets of downtown New York, in a constant state of admiration. Amazed by the immense "palaces" of Broadway, Loos became to me the Walt Whitman of lower Manhattan.

Is it really necessary to add that Adolf Loos is the founder of our "tradition of expatriates"—as we have always been called and always will be—in the same way as Henry James was for literature? Travellers moving more through time than through space. To illustrate this attitude better, I would need to introduce Henry James and speculate on the rather peculiar function he had in regard to what is usually known as *Generation perdue* but this would be a significant detour from the topic under investigation.

What I can briefly say that this living condition, this tradition of the vagabond lost within an immense space; it was, it still is, a tradition of artists who in fact needed to get away from themselves in the first place. In this Loos was similar to Hemingway or James. And who but Loos could have succeeded in putting several feet of twilight between his life and his art? Oskar Kokoschka said that "knowing Loos was an experience that determined one's fate." With the science of hindsight, I can include Schindler and myself among such a group. Loos's tribute to America, combined with the passion we shared for ground-gripping shoes, was the force that motivated both of us to come here.

Not only have I done all these things, I have also meditated about their meaning. Yet this was not, of course, just my story. It was, in fact, a wide spread transatlantic condition. What I want to say here is that, all our choices, individually made, to settle in Europe or America (depending on which side one was on) and to make our career there, represents the relevant point. These choices, including those of James and Loos at the beginning, are emblematic. In several respects they manifest themselves as a characteristically "modern" undertaking. They express the individuality of the personages involved, their thoughtfulness about themselves, their efficiency in execution, and a judgment upon their hometown.

Here I have to stop. This is my account. Of course, one can argue that my picture, in this form, is highly exaggerated. But there are advantages. It may be through examples such as these that one could begin to understand the concept of "voluntary exiles." But, to throw a last question in the picture, was this an historical necessity? In retrospect, it is indeed an historical necessity if this condition was promptly understood—and one may even say discovered—by Adolf

Loos exactly 400 years after Columbus. One may even go so far as to say that, in fact, before being Adolf Loos, Adolf Loos was Columbus himself. Like Columbus, Loos sighted America, the real America. Like Columbus, Loos had been affected by a tragic personal destiny.

The discovery of a "New World" made him excited about it to the point of going back to his native country to widely advertise the significance of his discovery tragically believing in his ability to change, via his knowledge, the lives of Viennese; at least as much as his discovery changed his. That he eventually succeeded in doing so in the long run, and provoked countless series of transatlantic crossings, it is just another joke of history, or, in other words, a case of posthumous fame which is rare and the least desired of all items: since the one who stood most to profit is dead and hence it is not for sale. But this is another topic altogether, and I am running late. Since I started by saying that I wanted to balance the budget of architectural accounts in the 20th century, and I began to do so, I can only conclude by noting that last week's cover of the *New Yorker* featured a sort of Purgatory mountain where those politicians who promised to cut taxes and balance the budget were burning in the hottest *girone dei dannati*. Since I have tried to fulfil my initial promise, I can only hope that you will not place me there

Printed in Italy
by PressUP, Nepi (VT)